M000249971

Palgrave Studies in Democracy, Innovation, and Entrepreneurship for Growth

Series Editor
Elias G. Carayannis
The George Washington University
Washington, District of Columbia, USA

The central theme of this series is to explore why some areas grow and others stagnate, and to measure the effects and implications in a trans-disciplinary context that takes both historical evolution and geographical location into account. In other words, when, how and why does the nature and dynamics of a political regime inform and shape the drivers of growth and especially innovation and entrepreneurship? In this socio-economic and socio-technical context, how could we best achieve growth, financially and environmentally?

This series aims to address such issues as:

- How does technological advance occur, and what are the strategic processes and institutions involved?
- How are new businesses created? To what extent is intellectual property protected?
- Which cultural characteristics serve to promote or impede innovation? In what ways is wealth distributed or concentrated?

These are among the key questions framing policy and strategic decision-making at firm, industry, national, and regional levels.

A primary feature of the series is to consider the dynamics of innovation and entrepreneurship in the context of globalization, with particular respect to emerging markets, such as China, India, Russia, and Latin America. (For example, what are the implications of China's rapid transition from providing low-cost manufacturing and services to becoming an innovation powerhouse? How do the perspectives of history and geography explain this phenomenon?)

Contributions from researchers in a wide variety of fields will connect and relate the relationships and inter-dependencies among (1) Innovation, (2) Political Regime, and (3) Economic and Social Development. We will consider whether innovation is demonstrated differently across sectors (e.g., health, education, technology) and disciplines (e.g., social sciences, physical sciences), with an emphasis on discovering emerging patterns, factors, triggers, catalysts, and accelerators to innovation, and their impact on future research, practice, and policy.

This series will delve into what are the sustainable and sufficient growth mechanisms for the foreseeable future for developed, knowledge-based economies and societies (such as the EU and the US) in the context of multiple, concurrent and inter-connected "tipping-point" effects with short (MENA) as well as long (China, India) term effects from a geo-strategic, geo-economic, geo-political and geo-technological set of perspectives.

This conceptualization lies at the heart of the series, and offers to explore the correlation between democracy, innovation and growth.

More information about this series at
http://www.springer.com/series/14635

Halvor Holtskog • Elias G. Carayannis
Aris Kaloudis • Geir Ringen

Learning Factories

The Nordic Model of Manufacturing

Halvor Holtskog
Department of Manufacturing
and Civil Engineering
Norwegian University of Science
and Technology
Gjøvik, Norway

Aris Kaloudis
Department of Industrial Economics
and Technology Management
Norwegian University of Science
and Technology
Gjøvik, Norway

Elias G. Carayannis
School of Business
George Washington University
Washington, District of Columbia, USA

Geir Ringen
Department of Manufacturing
and Civil Engineering
Norwegian University of Science
and Technology
Gjøvik, Norway

Palgrave Studies in Democracy, Innovation, and Entrepreneurship for Growth
ISBN 978-3-319-41886-5   ISBN 978-3-319-41887-2   (eBook)
https://doi.org/10.1007/978-3-319-41887-2

Library of Congress Control Number: 2017953060

© The Editor(s) (if applicable) and The Author(s) 2018
This work is subject to copyright. All rights are solely and exclusively licensed by the Publisher, whether the whole or part of the material is concerned, specifically the rights of translation, reprinting, reuse of illustrations, recitation, broadcasting, reproduction on microfilms or in any other physical way, and transmission or information storage and retrieval, electronic adaptation, computer software, or by similar or dissimilar methodology now known or hereafter developed.
The use of general descriptive names, registered names, trademarks, service marks, etc. in this publication does not imply, even in the absence of a specific statement, that such names are exempt from the relevant protective laws and regulations and therefore free for general use. The publisher, the authors and the editors are safe to assume that the advice and information in this book are believed to be true and accurate at the date of publication. Neither the publisher nor the authors or the editors give a warranty, express or implied, with respect to the material contained herein or for any errors or omissions that may have been made. The publisher remains neutral with regard to jurisdictional claims in published maps and institutional affiliations.

Cover Illustration: © Nina Matthews / Alamy Stock

Printed on acid-free paper

This Palgrave Macmillan imprint is published by Springer Nature
The registered company is Springer International Publishing AG
The registered company address is: Gewerbestrasse 11, 6330 Cham, Switzerland

CONTENTS

LIST OF FIGURES

LIST OF TABLES

CHAPTER 1

Introductory Chapter

Abstract This chapter aims to provide deeper insight into how a modern and sophisticated management of employees plays an important and—in our view—key role for the successful reindustrialization of the Western world. There are important lessons to learn from high-cost countries that successfully compete in the global marketplace. In such contexts, the re-combination of tacit knowledge, people, competences and culture to create effective and efficient automated production is indeed essential.

INTRODUCTION

In both the USA and Europe, there are currently huge efforts to reindustrialize economies after decades of neglecting industry as the most important economic factor for society. Such a phenomenon is the starting point of this investigation. Specifically, Japanese ways of production have often been studied and—to some degree—copied by American and European firms whereby 'Lean' has become the de facto standard for effective and efficient production. Recently, however, new initiatives have emerged. Industry 4.0 is one of these, and it has a strong technological focus. It involves censors which gather data from every step of the automated production process, identifying each nut and bolt is prerequisite, as is the usage of big data. However, little attention is given to people and the knowledge-creation process.

© The Author(s) 2018
H. Holtskog et al., *Learning Factories*, Palgrave Studies in Democracy, Innovation, and Entrepreneurship for Growth, https://doi.org/10.1007/978-3-319-41887-2_1

This book aims to provide deeper insight into how the people-aspect plays an important and—in our view—key role for the successful reindustrialization of the Western world. It argues that there are important learning points from high cost countries that successfully compete in the global marketplace. In such contexts, the re-combination of tacit knowledge, people, and culture to create effective and efficient automated production is indeed essential and visible.

The Norwegian labor market and work organization are similar to those of Denmark and Sweden, its Nordic neighbors. This socio-economic organization is often labeled 'the *Nordic model*,' the result of four key institutionalized societal mechanisms:

- Centrally led wage negotiations between trade unions and employer federations
- Safety nets of health insurance, welfare benefits, and pensions to all citizens
- Labor market flexibility, that is, a high degree of job mobility and career experimentation combined with a high degree of job safety
- Democratic decision processes and high employee participation in organizing work tasks at all levels

This book claims that the above-mentioned mechanisms produce a specific style of collaboration and learning at work which significantly differs from work organization styles observed more generally in the European Union (EU), UK, USA, Japan, or elsewhere. We empirically examine the strengths, tensions, and challenges that the work organization style meets in the automotive industry—probably the most globalized industry in the world.

The automotive industry provides precisely the type of business environment that allows studies of how work organization practices—partly shaped by strictly defined legislation and centrally negotiated rules—adjust to global economic forces and mechanisms. Yet, precisely what types of tensions and redefinitions of work practices and styles do we observe when learning in a Norwegian automotive company that meets the global marketplace?

Moreover, there is another—equally important—rationale for writing this book. In many developed countries, the question of *reindustrializing* the economy is becoming extremely important. Societal and economic spillovers from manufacturing industries are now better understood, and there is the increasing awareness of the fact that competitive, modern economies require strong manufacturing sectors as the precondition for globally competitive services. Thus, this book enlightens such a discussion by examining how aspects of the Nordic model create competitive advantages in high-cost countries such as Norway. We argue on the evidence provided in this book that a democratic, flexible, and adaptive organizational form of learning is an important contributing factor to the creation of competitive advantage.

As we live in a world that is steadily becoming more globalized and interactive, the business environment has evolved to become more globally orientated and competitive. Such changes have led to more rapid technological development as well as changes in the societies where the companies operate. Therefore, capabilities that companies rely on must be designed in a way that can keep up with this rapid transformation in a globalized world (Levinthal, 2009). These capabilities include organizational knowledge, or what the organization knows and can use in its operations, in order to be successful (Dosi, Nelson, & Winter, 2009) and form competitive advantage: 'The importance of knowledge as a key source of competitive advantages is now well established in management studies' (Nonaka & Nishiguchi, 2001, p. 3). This strategy tradition focuses on management and how new management ideas, processes, and organizational design can become strategic resources (Argyres, Felin, Foss, & Zenger, 2012). In addition, Argyres et al. (2012) demonstrate that management possesses the most valuable knowledge, supporting the top-down approach to its spreading. Garicano and Wu (2012) agree on this when they conclude that task orientation informs how knowledge is acquired. Specifically, task orientation concentrates on what each employee should and must learn in order to do a good job; the management of tasks is therefore essential along with building a knowledge hierarchy.

In many ways, Norwegian work–life research contrasts this strategic view of organizational management. Here, the roots of the tradition are firmly placed in human relations, where democratic and broad direct participation of all organizational levels dominate thinking (Gustavsen, Finne, & Oscarsson, 2001; Johnsen, 2001; Klev & Levin, 2009; Røvik, 1998). This tradition argues that autonomy in teams will bring innovation ideas from the employees from the bottom-up, termed 'employee-driven innovation' (EDI) (Pedersen, 2012). Central to EDI is that '*learning can produce innovation*' and there is a '*complex interplay of processes that include factors at the individual level as well as organizational culture*' (Pedersen, 2012, p. 4). Its motivation is captured in the following statement by Kesting and Ulhøi (2010, p. x): '*Employees typically acquire exclusive and in-depth and highly context-dependent knowledge that managers often do not possess.'* Essentially, these authors posit that EDI-thinking occurs within two organizational roles: management and employees. And, although they highlight the need for close collaboration between the roles, the dichotomy remains. Further, high technological development creates exclusive and in-depth context-dependent knowledge (ibid.). However, employees working daily in the context, with the technology-like automated machines and so on, hold no such knowledge.

This book holds on to the Norwegian work–life tradition and importance of EDI, but it has a different viewpoint. In matrix organizations, the organizational roles are more diffused. A person can be both a leader and an employee in the same company, or one can have many bosses. In this understanding, the dichotomy makes little sense. Rather than holding on to the roles of employee–management, this book begins differently. Organizing product development projects, according to the matrix principle, is common (Cooper & Edgett, 2005; Morgan & Liker, 2006; Nishiguchi, 1996; Ottoson, 2010). Aligning to this principle, this book considers *how industries create knowledge*. Learning and innovation in such advanced organizational structures require some special foundations to be effective and efficient. Learning requires a special kind of leadership in the sense of leader roles and the ability to facilitate the learning process among organizational members. Further, organizational culture plays an important role in learning, and the structure and tools are the final dimensions. This multi-dimensional framework creates better understanding, increasing insight into how technologically and organizationally advanced companies learn and create knowledge in effective and efficient ways. This is, of course, based on high employee involvement using the context-dependent knowledge.

From a system perspective, this book is also important. Supplier companies are subsystems of various OEMs,[1] and these companies too are composed of multiple subsystems. Therefore, the challenge of management is to manage complex relations between subsystems within subsystems without having the company fall apart, adding yet another complication to the organizational learning model.

ASSUMPTIONS AND THEORETICAL FRAMEWORK

This way of thinking is inspired by Cartesian doubt—thoughts form the epistemological foundation for the individual's knowledge. However, Cartesius posed that there is always some skepticism present and doubt therefore becomes an effort to defeat such knowledge bases. Specifically, three distinct levels of doubt exist: perceptual illusion, the dream problem, and the deceiving God ('Descartes: God and Human Nature,' 2013). 'Perceptual illusion' means that our senses can play with us. Magicians are experts in illusion and the audience becomes astonished when impossible things happen on stage. In everyday life, our senses play a vital role in how we perceive things, but many times what we perceive turns out to be something else, such as often the case for first impressions. 'The dream problem' refers to the boundary between a dream-state and consciousness that can be difficult to separate. Psychology has proven that the human brain fills in blank spots and creates patterns. These pattern recognitions are well developed (Lehrer, 2012). However, this does not mean that the patterns, or the creative process, produce something close to what many regard as reality. 'A deceiving God' in Cartesian philosophy invites us to doubt our traditional beliefs. In his case, it was religion. Systematic doubt challenges existing knowledge and makes us rethink initial thoughts. In this way, new aspects are discovered. With a system perspective, or subsystems within subsystems, such doubt drives the investigation by assuming the conclusions are wrong which therefore creates the motivation to test them. In social science, systematic doubt is pursued in triangulation because it is void of laboratory control that allows us to refine the range. Therefore, the alternative is to look at something from various angles and hope to discover something about it.

Flick pointed out that qualitative research often focuses on multi-methods (Denzin & Lincoln, 1994; Flick, 1998, p. 229). The metaphor triangulation comes from military usage and naval navigation where multiple reference points were used to pinpoint, through geometry, the exact position of an object (Smith & Kleine, 1986). Thus, '[t]*he combination of multiple methodological practices, empirical materials, perspectives, and observers in a single study is best understood, then, as a strategy that adds rigor, breadth, complexity, richness, and depth to any inquiry*' (Flick, 1998, p. 231). One common misconception is that triangulation is used in social science to check and validate studies. Indeed, achieving consistency across data sources or methods can be useful, although Patton (2002) argued that inconsistencies reveal opportunities to uncover deeper meaning in the data. The same argument can be found in Miles and Huberman's book, *Qualitative Data Analysis* (Miles & Huberman, 1994, pp. 266–267).

Another support for the argument of uncovering deeper meaning in the data is offered by Yeasmin and Rahman (2012). These authors point out that triangulation tends to support interdisciplinary research, where theories from different disciplines help deepen our understandings, arguing for triangulation as something natural to humans and a common way of thinking. Alternatively, '[t]*here may be a correspondence between life as lived, life as experienced, and life as told, but the anthropologist should never assume the correspondence, or fail to make the distinction*' (Bruner & Plattner, 1984, p. 7). Not only should anthropologists never assume or fail to make such distinctions, all social scientists should keep this in mind.

Additionally, social research may use the mix method (Tashakkori & Teddlie, 2010). Here, one core project investigates a problem by analyzing different data using one strategy, supplementing this with another strategy that provides access to other data, but still explains the same phenomenon. The first and supplemental strategy will go into the same publication (Morse, 2010, p. 340). It is different from multi-method or multi-dimensional analysis, where each supplementary strategy can be published on its own with the overall picture often published in synthesized articles.

This book uses multi-dimensional analysis and method, relating to its epistemological and ontological foundations. What we everyday call reality is in fact our own versions or perceptions of things that happen around us. With a business world becoming more globalized and interactive, the system perspective of subsystems within subsystems indicates the complexities of reality. Dealing with such complexity, no single perspective can truly describe it. Or, in other words, triangulation is necessary because of the multiple causal chains that compose human life.

A combination of the basic triangulation types is argued as ideal (Denzin, 1970, 2009). Here, multi-dimensional analysis combines different types and data sources are triangulated relating to the three variables of space, time, and person. When personal data sources are used, the collective and interactive levels are focused upon. For this book, there were several researchers involved in the two companies, and many reflection seminars and meetings were held. However, there are no specific records of who reflected on what and who contributed with which insight. Methodological triangulation is conducted through interviews (formal and informal), observation, participation, surveys, and company documents. As for theory, three are used as framing perspectives, organizational learning (Argyris & Schön, 1996), organizational culture (Martin, 1992), and facilitative management (Hirschhorn, 1997). Using these different perspectives to describe product development projects in matrix organizations minimizes the suppression of contradictory explanations and brings deeper insight into the complex process of creating knowledge and learning in an industrial setting. Precisely, it is like looking into a kaleidoscope and finding new pictures of changing facets and colors.

Therefore, the argument is a combination of political economy, social organization, and cultural systems (classification, worldviews, ideologies, and myth) together make a framework for the analysis of a human system. However, the multi-method perspective here is limited to organizational behavior and technology management. Therefore, this book investigates organizational behaviors with multi-causalities within multi-dimensional nested systems, guiding the theoretical positions.

THEORETICAL FOUNDATION

Manufacturing industries have created many reforms for maintaining and developing their efficiency and effectiveness. Both quality and Lean[2] systems have lots of initiatives and tools for formalizing the work method used at different levels in the organization. Further, they also have initiatives and tools for tapping into the tacit knowledge of the workers, motivating continuous improvement. Ideally, workers should continually come up with ways of improving work to develop best practice by formalizing how a task is done, for example, with one-point lessons. These are distributed throughout the company when changed. In this way, the company's operations become more efficient and effective throughout the years.

Concurrently, these reforms also implement overall operational systems such as just-in-time, statistical process control, and so on. Such systems demand specific structures and prescribe distinct methods to gain overall results. Klein (1989, 1991) places these arguments together in two articles, where the loss of autonomy regarding performance and method are central points. These losses are scaled toward individuals and teams. However, the companies also loose autonomy of decisions. For instance, just-in-time set the production pace for all of the subcontractors delivering parts. This means that scales of autonomy, performance, and method can be used to describe development in a bigger picture. In this book, Fig. 1.1 guides the argumentation:

The four quadrats represent different ways of conducting work or doing business. Ideally, a company can decide its own performance, for instance, how many products it produces and of what quality, and which production method. However, in reality the company serves a market, and it is the market that decides the volume and/or level of quality alongside its competitors.

Fig. 1.1 The guiding argumentation

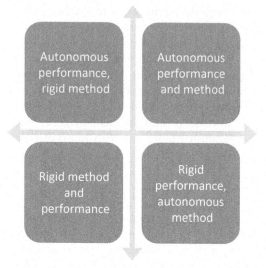

These factors—market and competitors—influence the production method. The method is seldom something that company can autonomously decide.

Mirroring these choices is the conduct of internal operations. Ideally, production teams should be autonomous in their performance and method, but due to automation, tight coordination with other teams on the production line, and so on, performance tends to be more rigid. Additionally, the previous autonomous methods may suffer due to more automation, standards, and production reforms.

DATA USAGE

Data were gathered from two case studies including formal documents, in-depth interviews, participation, observations, and surveys. Different approaches to the case studies have been followed. Case 1 (C6) is the main study where the research team tried to facilitate different changes and followed a specific development project in detail over a period of two years. Meanwhile, Case 2 (C3) is the secondary case where another researcher initiated some of the change processes. These change efforts have been primarily in the quality department and were therefore not included in this book. In C3, data were gathered by talking to various people and looking at some internal data from systems, serving as the validation tool and correction point for C6 in an effort to supplement and deepen reflection. In total, each researcher[3] had over 200 interactions with people in the two companies, with the frequency of at least three to four days a week; three researchers working with C6 and two with C3. In total, we spoke to 32 different people at C6 and over 51 at C3. These people represent every position in C6, as well as the most important ones for research and development at C3. Adding to the interactions with the case companies, one member of the research team held several managerial positions at C6, and another was deeply involved in establishing the managerial system at C6. When the financial crisis struck, the researchers became involved in writing applications for the funding of development projects in both companies. The work yielded valuable insight into the economic side of these, providing us with information that we could not have elsewhere gotten. Holding the position of chair, consultant, and local resident made it easier to initiate reflection processes in the case companies, putting us in the unique position to facilitate—or manage—some sort of reflection 'orchestration' (Göranzon, Hammarén, & Ennals, 2004).

A Short Description of the Data

Survey #1 is a survey that was targeted toward the Norwegian automotive industry's development departments. It had 123 respondents in 19 different companies, with seven of them located in Raufoss.[4] The general idea behind the survey was to acquire insight into how development departments work in this globally advanced industry. It consisted of 81 questions which were grouped according to competence, decisions and teams, planning and control, formal processes, motivation and leadership, information flow, continuous learning, understanding the customer, entrepreneurship, external resources, and set-based concurrent engineering. Each question required an answer on a Likert scale from 1 to 5.

The formal written documents are written on the different systems in the case companies. The research group had full access to every system at C6, as well as the most interesting ones at C3.[5] Data from these systems were primarily from the quality and management system, for example, the different versions of Failure Mode and Effects Analysis (FMEA) were formed together over the lifetime of the followed development project.

The operative research team, which consisted of three people, was given access to follow the development of a new suspension part for a North European car manufacturer (the main case). We began our work some time before the contract was achieved, and followed it to the planning of the industrialization phase. Sitting in many of the project meetings, both internally and externally, the quality expert in the team was also used as regular help in the project.

The observation of change actions[6] was taken out of the participation to demonstrate that we tried to change in our effort via action research. We attempted to simplify the FMEA process and form, which C6 thought was a very good idea and took charge of with the quality expert as a consultant. We further tried to make the project's progress and problem-solving more visual. Toyota has something called the Obeya room (big room) where everything important to a project is put up for every participant to see. We tried this at C6, but there were no rooms to do this so we settled for a movable whiteboard, and brought it to every meeting. The idea was that we should start updating the whiteboard and gradually leave the responsibility to the company. However, in practice, this did not fully work, as we were the only ones updating the board. And, upon discussing its value several times with no update actions, the idea was abandoned.[7] Another idea was the A3 form, or focus sheet as we called it (Shook, 2008; Sobek & Smalley, 2008). This followed the same idea of visualizing the problems, thus making it easier to contribute to the problem-solving process. Based on data from specific parts of the development project, the research team produced several A3 forms demonstrating the technique. In some ways, it was adapted, such as when the project manager made some forms to show his colleagues about a specific problem, although the majority did not use them. The observation of change actions became much more focused on when the financial crisis struck and the organizational changes started. Volunteerism or 'dugnad' was partially prominent. The new leadership wanted to withdraw C6 from the research project, but then the developers stepped in and told management about the value of the research team. An agreement was reached about further participation in the project of development of parts to the North European car manufacturer.

In-depth interviews were conducted for two purposes: (a) to familiarize with the employees in their professional work and workplace, and (b) to attain insight into specific problems. When asked, everyone took time off to speak with us, and these conversations could sometimes last for much longer than planned due to long technological explanations. There were also some people who travelled a lot and were seldom in the office and getting them to talk required more creative approaches. For example, there is a travel office that coordinates travel at the Raufoss Industrial

Park, and one of its services is car rental to-and-from the airport which takes approximately 1.5 hours. We were able to coordinate our travel in the same rental car.

Participation represents taking an active part in discussions and meetings, as well as widening the research team's knowledge. In-depth interviews were also used to check and clarify our understandings of the technological details. When the financial crisis struck the case companies, a new opportunity emerged for writing public-funding applications of R&D projects. Writing these meant that, as a research team, we had even more time to talk with the experts, obtaining more insight into what they believed were cutting-edge technologies and why. This contributed to facilitating a deeper understanding of the companies, especially regarding the inner—or more hidden—logic of the engineering culture and its tools.

A network survey was conducted of explaining the rules element from which we produced a networking survey. We collected collaboration data by asking the project members who they talked with and how often. In addition, we mapped which external people arose in this exercise, as well as their colleagues and specialties. What is presented in this book is a simplification of these data. Nevertheless, during this phase many contacts between the North European car manufacturer as the customer and C6 occurred. The project leader and the sales and marketing manager at C6 verified the chart. The findings were presented to the sales and marketing manager, and the development manager at C3. C3, though, had a slightly different system with onsite engineers[8] who stay in constant direct contact with the customer, but once a project is under way, the contact patterns were very similar to that of C6.

Investigations were first characterized by getting to know the various systems, standards, and formal documentation at C6. Lots of formal documents were read, and a pattern gradually emerged that did not correspond with the formal systems. All the formal documents, notes, in-depth interviews, and forms were gradually built in a database using NVivo[9] which served as a repository for coded data used for analysis and reflections.

VALIDITY

Guba and Lincoln (1989) frame validity as a matter of both credibility and authenticity, defining credibility as '*the idea … of isomorphism between constructed realities of respondents and the reconstructions attributed to them*' (pp. 236–237). The verification of such an isomorphism can be conducted through several techniques (pp. 237–250) which will now be looked upon in light of the research project.

Prolonged Engagement This is substantial involvement in the field or case. The research team stayed close to the companies involved in this project over a period of four years, and some of the members had previous experience with them in other projects. Therefore, it is natural to argue that there are minimal effects of misinformation, distortion, or fronts. We tried to facilitate our immersion in and understanding of the context's culture. However, due to the financial crisis our engagement took a different turn than initially planned. It started with a change of CEO at the main case company (C6), an Austrian, who wanted to withdraw C6 from the research project. He argued that people in the organization needed to concentrate on their actual work. However, the R&D department strongly argued that they wanted to stay because it was valuable to them in terms of gaining deeper insight into quality and management systems, as well as improvements in development processes. C6 remained in the research project where the focus was on a specific development of a suspension part for the North European car manufacturer. Soon, other tasks engaged the research team, such as applying for more public funding.

Persistent Observation This adds depth to the scope that prolonged engagement affords. The research team had access to quality and management systems, as well as to the network disks where temporary files and forms were placed during their completion process. These formal systems meant that we could check assumptions and statements from the participants in the case companies. We also had available data from the operation's management logging system which allowed us to establish the success of each production process and enabled us to go back many years. The manual paper-based achievement was subjected to scrutiny in some of our investigations. As for observation, we participated in many of the various project meetings in the development of parts to the North European car manufacturer. Further, as the research team consisted of four people, observed phenomena could be discussed and reflected upon from different angles.

Peer Debriefing The purpose here is to test the findings with someone directly involved in the situation and to highlight tacit and implicit information. The research has accomplished this in various ways. First, supervisors and the staff at EDWOR[10] have been a great help by indicating the various theoretical directions that could contain different explanatory powers for the field observations. Second, findings were discussed with two experienced people working at Raufoss who held PhD degrees. These discussions have added depth to the findings. Third, one of the research team members had previously worked at C6 as both a production and quality manager and was now involved in research of the quality system. His insights and knowledge of C6 and its people were very helpful, and we set up routine weekly debriefings which were extremely helpful as we were not able to gather large or small groups for common reflection purposes, as described in the co-generative model. These debriefs often resulted in questions about assumptions to be asked to specific individuals in the R&D department and/or things to be checked in the formal systems.

Negative Case Analysis This is the analogue to a statistical test for quantitative data. We began the workshop with the intention that this should be followed up with more dialogue conferences where our reasoning would be tested and problems could find solutions. However, as previously mentioned, the financial crisis struck, and we had to think differently. Both findings and our assumptions were presented to the various managers at the companies and corrected as appropriate. This was not a fully negative case analysis, although some effort to test the findings and assumptions were made given the special circumstances. We had to be quite creative to speak to every person involved in the development project, for example, the airport trips shared with some of the busiest people which offered the possibility of 100% focus over a 1.5-hour period.

Progressive Subjectivity This is the process of monitoring the evaluator's development of constructions and the degree of privilege making one's own a priori assumptions dominate. The research started out by writing a research proposal for admission to the EDWOR program which was based on the goals and objectives of the research project (already underway), but set into a social science perspective. The EDWOR program was specifically designed for doing research in the field and dealing with specific research topics generated from the field itself. The EDWOR program has been called a 'travelling circus' (Ennals, 2006, p. 310) where intensive teaching for four weeks a year occurs at different locations. The intensity of this learning pressures the students, myself included, to be well prepared, leading to many becoming frustrated. However, the frustration was the inspiration to dig deeper into theory and make greater research reflections.[11]

The first research question when entering the EDWOR program was how product developers could be both creative and Lean (effective and efficient) at the same time.[12] This seemed to be a paradox because product development was described as a group effort, and according to democratic values, everyone needs to be heard. Adding to this knowledge, there is much writing about the democratic, participatory actions in companies according to the Norwegian work–life research tradition. Therefore, the supervisors challenged us to write about this using the eyes of different theories relating to: knowledge management, transaction cost economics, market strategic thinking, trust, the Nordic Network Model, and open innovation. Some of these thoughts transcended into a book chapter (Holtskog, 2013) about the Lean perspective versus the findings of the Enterprise Development 2000 project. One of the supervisors, a professor at Gjøvik University College[13] who has worked for more than a decade in the Raufoss clusters in various issues, challenged us to think differently. He constantly pushed our understanding of technology, and how our suggested solutions and understandings could work in the case companies. Our a priori assumptions were challenged, both theoretically and more practically (the workability), by several people. And, of all the suggested practical suggestions, workability became a mantra.

Workability as the main guideline and focus creates two outcomes. First, it can guide the researcher to become more subjective in his or her observations and thinking. Specifically, it is easy to be fascinated by the seemingly well-thought-out and argued systems and procedures in the case companies. Therefore, the effort is to contribute to making these better where inefficiencies are discovered. This thinking can lead to a celebration of the already installed systems and procedures. Second, it can lead to a much deeper knowledge base for the researcher to make critical reflections. The research team member, who had worked at C6 before, began with a basis of the first outcome, but was corrected by the other members and gradually became more critical. We also encountered that the development project team encouraged us to have a critical stance toward the present way of doing things.

Member Checks This deals with hypotheses testing, data, preliminary categories, and interpretation with the members of the community from which the constructions are collected. Formal interviews were transcribed and sent to the respondent for approval, while only some informal interviews were transcribed; most were just written as notes in shared personal research journals. Still, the meaning and assumptions drawn from these notes were cross-checked with other members in the companies, as no meaning or assumptions are included without this step. Cross-checking was also applied to project meetings, focus groups, and hallway conversations in addition to some written material and recorded data in the management or quality systems. The research team has taken great precaution to avoid factual and interpretive errors. Unfortunately, we were not able to put together a large group of people working at the development department to discuss our findings due to the exceptional situation caused in the wake of the financial crisis and the fact that the new CEO did not approve of spending time this way. Additionally, some of the managers were extremely busy and appointments were hard to get, though one of the creative ways to be able to spend some time with them was to drive with them to the airport, which was done a total of six times.

Unfortunately, collective reflection suffered in the wake of the financial crisis. We were not able to have large meetings where important topics and insights would have been shared and discussed. Nevertheless, we believe that the sheer number of interactions, as well as being a part of the professional community over such a long time will—to some extent—make up for this disadvantage.

Transferability (External Validity) The research was conducted with C6 as the main focal point and case, but C3 was visited often to establish if there were some similarities and/or correct understandings. One member in the four-person research team only worked with C3. In this way, she was the contact point, making comparisons easier. Both companies compete in the global automotive industry and are relatively large in Norway. We did not check if our findings could be transferred to medium- or small-sized companies or to see if they were transferable to other industries, although much of our general understanding and theories were developed by investigating the automotive industry. However, investigating cultural systems highlights diversity, although the collection of ongoing sense-making activities by the members provides the basis for common understanding that can be transferred to other organizations. The rich description of diversity is offered for managers to understand this as organizational strength to which they can enact upon (Greenwood, 1991).

Dependability This is about the stability of the data over time. Specifically, this research was conducted at the outbreak, duration, and recovery phase of the financial crisis,[14] with lots of stress and uncertainty noticeable in the case companies. C3 was sold to one of the world's biggest car-parts manufacturers, and C6 had financial problems. Thus, both firms made redundancies and organizational changes. To imply that this did not affect the research would be wrong. Yet, we described the situation (Holtskog, Ringen, & Endrerud, 2010), and found that despite the lay-offs, workload in the development departments increased.[15] Nevertheless, as this book is about industrial learning, the crisis made findings clearer. More activity with fewer people meant that they had to work more efficiently and effectively. People working in the development project were under a huge amount of pressure to carry it out because it was thought to be vital to C6's survival, yet at the same time, the North European car manufacturer prevented their developers from traveling to Norway and C6 did not travel much to Sweden. This meant that most discussions were by phone, phone conferences, or e-mails which made keeping track easier than if we were briefed after an actor's journey to Sweden.

Confirmability This assures that the data, interpretations, and inquiry outcomes are rooted in the proper contexts. As we had access to the data system, cross-checking made this auditing for confirmability relatively easy. The entire focus of the research project and book is on the Norwegian automotive industry at Raufoss, although there are other types of industries such as defense, water, and gas that are not accounted for here.

The Authenticity Criteria Fairness did somehow suffer as in other circumstances, we could arrange a more democratic process of reflection, thereby tapping into the potential of more open reflections from the participants. In this regard, the educative authenticity also suffered as only a small amount of resources could be used for organizational learning in terms of the different ways of thinking and doing things. The ontological authenticity is more accounted for as we changed specific quality and problem-solving processes (such as FMEA and A3) when highlighting some hidden negative sides of the present practice. Some efforts were made to make the catalytic authenticity of daily reflections easier. One example was the whiteboard setup near the coffee machine to display current challenges and problems. The idea was that people could take a pen and draw or write a contribution for a possible solution, although this was not done entirely as intended. Another thing was to ease the implementation of Ford's[16] quality system and bring production process data into the discussions which helped overcome some of the assumptions that the powerful and experienced people had insisted on. These actions were picked up by people at C6 and were further refined. The last point, tactical authenticity, was never felt to be a problem in relation to the crisis as we—as a research team—could acquire all the information needed for our task. The general sense the team had was that this was also true for the people working at C6, and if a bright idea came up, they acted on it.

All in all, the research was conducted as best as possible according to the validity and authenticity criteria of Guba and Lincoln (1989), as well as the credibility criteria of Greenwood (1991) and Levinthal (2009).

The overall structure of the book is as follows.

Chapter 2—The financial crisis and Norwegian automotive industry. This chapter explores the reasons why the Norwegian industry performed well during the financial crisis and the general lessons that can be learned from this. This is the result an extensive survey investigating how the economic crisis resulted in increased efficiency and effectiveness in Norwegian manufacturing. It paves the way for the remainder of the book by asking how such positive results can emerge out of a crisis. The chapter also discusses how to extrapolate findings from the Norwegian case to a global context. Interestingly, the first part of the survey was completed before the financial crisis, and the second in its aftermath, offering a unique perspective.

Chapter 3—Development of suspension parts project. From the crisis perspective, this chapter focuses on the specificities of a development project in the automation industry. The chapter introduces the reader to product development in the industry, demonstrating how the organization learns (or not) from project to project. This descriptive approach as to how product development occurs presents a reality, which is in stark contrast to the one presented in the firms' formal description of quality management systems and other types of formal displays.

Chapter 4—Organizational Culture—The Differentiated perspective. As the previous chapter discussed sectoral aspects of knowledge and value creation, this chapter focuses on the micro level, i.e., level of firm. It shows how global manufacturing/managerial trends, sectoral specific factors, national contexts, and firm specific features are represented into firms' cultural aspects. The analysis provides the deeper understanding of subcultures and their respective behaviors in a manufacturing context.

Chapter 5—Culture—Internal business contradictions. This chapter broadens and deepens insight made by bringing in another theoretical perspective: the Geertzian perspective of culture. It describes how broader global managerial trends affect knowledge creation processes and the differentiated cultures they are embedded in.

Chapter 6—Facilitative management. This chapter reflects upon the previous by identifying the key skills and sensitivities that good management teams within modern manufacturing companies should possess. Given the complexities and variability of modern manufacturing production lines and markets, the management teams must ensure they act in a facilitative manner, that is, to be able to intelligently tap into and act upon cultural understanding to unleash the creative forces and eagerness of learning embedded in the organization.

Chapter 7—Implications for reindustrialization of advanced economies. This chapter looks into different efforts to reindustrialize Europe. We review three broad policy agendas in order to identify how modern policy thinking conceives the issue of reindustrialization and what type of threats and opportunities are perceived as important in this context. The chapter ends by discussing these threats and opportunities according to the managerial implications.

Chapter 8—Conclusion. This chapter concludes by summing up and outlining the implications of the research, as well as the contributions to theory, policy, and practice. It returns the arguments to the meso and macro levels of the economy within the manufacturing sector. We argue that insights about facilitative management are key ingredients in securing conditions for a robust and competitive manufacturing sector in advanced economies. This way, we present an optimistic view and prospects as to how the advanced economies can sustain their competitiveness in balance with the qualities of their societies and democracies.

NOTES

1. OEM stands for Original Equipment Manufacturer such as Ford and General Motors.
2. Lean will be discussed in later chapters. It started as a way of explaining how the Japanese companies, especially Toyota, achieve high effectiveness and efficiency in their factories without compromising quality (Womack, Jones, & Roos, 1990).
3. Two of the researchers are authors of this book.
4. Where C6 and C3 are located.
5. As C3 has been listed on the Norwegian Stock Exchange and some information systems were closed to us, for example, the financial system.
6. The term *observation of actions* is used when the research team sat in on meetings and discussions, but did not actively participate. An observation

made on one member of the research group was shared with the others by discussions and reflection notes.

7. This is a common problem as people say it is very difficult to set aside time for reflections. It is another dimension of facilitative management but it is not the focus of this book.
8. On-site means working located at the customer's offices.
9. A much-used program for conducting social research; http://www.qsrinternational.com/products_nvivo.aspx
10. EDWOR program was the PhD-school at NTNU that one of the researchers attended. EDWOR stands for Enterprise Development and Work-Life Research.
11. Ennals' chapter describes how this EDWOR-program was conducted the first time around. It was very similar when the researcher participated in the EDWOR II program (2007).
12. This was in the research proposal written in the spring of 2007. Later, similar points were made by Isaksen and Kalsaas (2009).
13. Gjøvik University College is now a part of Norwegian University of Science and Technology (NTNU—www.ntnu.no).
14. The financial crisis was before the EURO crisis.
15. All the major companies at Raufoss Industrial Park participated in our investigation. See the context chapter for details.
16. Ford owned the North European car manufacturer at this point.

REFERENCES

Argyres, N., Felin, T., Foss, N., & Zenger, T. (2012). Organizational economics of capability and heterogeneity. *Organization Science, 23*(5), 1213–1226.

Argyris, C., & Schön, D. (1996). *Organizational learning II: Theory, method, and practice.* Reading: Addison-Wesley Publishing Company.

Bruner, E. M., & Plattner, S. (1984). *Text, play, and story: The construction and reconstruction of self and society: 1983 Proceedings of the American Ethnological Society.* Prospect Heights, IL: Waweland Press.

Cooper, R., & Edgett, S. (2005). *Lean, rapid and profitable New product development.* Ancaster: Product Development Institute.

Denzin, N. K. (1970). *The research act in sociology: A theoretical introduction to sociological methods.* London: Butterworths.

Denzin, N. K. (2009). *The research act: A theoretical introduction to sociological methods.* New Brunswick: Aldine Transaction.

Denzin, N. K., & Lincoln, Y. S. (1994). *Handbook of qualitative research.* Thousand Oaks, CA: Sage.

Descartes: God and Human Nature. (2013). Retrieved from http://www.philosophypages.com/hy/4d.htm

Dosi, G., Nelson, R. R., & Winter, S. G. (2009). *The nature and dynamics of organizational capabilities*. Oxford: Oxford University Press.

Ennals, J. R. (2006). Theatre and workplace actors. In B. Göranzon, M. Hammarén, & J. R. Ennals (Eds.), *Dialogue, skill & tacit knowledge* (pp. 307–319). West Sussex: John Wiley & Sons.

Flick, U. (1998). *An introduction to qualitative research: Theory, method and applications*. London: Sage.

Garicano, L., & Wu, Y. (2012). Knowledge, communication, and organizational capabilities. *Organization Science, 23*(5), 1382–1397.

Göranzon, B., Hammarén, M., & Ennals, J. R. (Eds.). (2004). *Dialogue, skill & tacit knowledge*. West Sussex: John Wiley & Sons.

Greenwood, D. J. (1991). Collective reflective practice through participatory action research: A case study from the Fagor cooperatives of Mondragón. In D. Schön (Ed.), *The reflective turn – Case studies in and on educational practice* (pp. 84–108). New York: Teachers College Press.

Guba, E. G., & Lincoln, Y. S. (1989). *Fourth generation evaluation*. Newbury Park, CA: Sage.

Gustavsen, B., Finne, H., & Oscarsson, B. (2001). *Creating connectedness: The role of social research in innovation policy*. Amsterdam: John Benjamins Publishing Company.

Hirschhorn, L. (1997). *Reworking authority: Leading and following in the post-modern organization*. Cambridge, MA: MIT Press.

Holtskog, H. (2013). Lean and innovative: Two discourses. In H. C. G. Johnsen & E. Pålshaugen (Eds.), *Hva er innovasjon? Perspektiver i norsk innovasjonsforskning. Bind 2: Organisasjon og medvirkning – en norsk modell?* (pp. 45–64). Oslo: Cappelen Damm Akademisk.

Holtskog, H., Ringen, G., & Endrerud, J. O. (2010). *Financial crisis affects absorptive capacity: Case Raufoss cluster*. Paper presented at the 5th International Seminar on Regional Innovation Policies, Grimstad, Norway.

Isaksen, A., & Kalsaas, B. T. (2009). Suppliers and strategies for upgrading in global production networks. The case of a supplier to the global automotive industry in a high-cost location. European Planning Studies, Special Edition.

Johnsen, H. (2001). *Involvement at work*. PhD, Copenhagen Business School, Copenhagen.

Kesting, P., & Ulhøi, J. P. (2010). Employee-driven innovation: Extending the license to foster innovation. *Management Decisions, 48*(1), 65–84.

Klein, J. A. (1989, March–April). The human cost of manufacturing reform. *Harvard Business Review, 60*–66.

Klein, J. A. (1991). A reexamination of autonomy in light of new manufacturing practices. *Human Relations, 44*(1), 21–38. https://doi.org/10.1177/001872679104400102

Klev, R., & Levin, M. (2009). *Forandring som praksis: endringsledelse gjennom læring og utvikling*. Bergen: Fagbokforl.

Lehrer, J. (2012). *Imagine: How creativity works.* Boston, MA: Houghton Mifflin Harcourt.

Levinthal, D. A. (2009). Organizational capabilities in complex worlds. In G. Dosi, P. R. Nelson, & S. G. Winter (Eds.), *The nature and dynamics of organizational capabilities* (pp. 363–379). Oxford: Oxford University Press.

Martin, J. (1992). *Cultures in organizations: Three perspectives.* New York: Oxford University Press.

Miles, H., & Huberman, M. (1994). *Qualitative data analysis: A sourcebook.* Beverly Hills, CA: Sage.

Morgan, J., & Liker, J. K. (2006). *The Toyota product development system, integrating people, process and technology.* New York: Productivity Press.

Morse, J. (2010). Procedures and practice of mix method design: Maintaining control, rigor, and complexity. In A. Tashakkori & C. Teddlie (Eds.), *SAGE handbook of mixed methods in social & behavioral research* (pp. 339–352). Thousand Oaks, CA: Sage.

Nishiguchi, T. E. (1996). *Managing product development.* New York: Oxford University Press.

Nonaka, I., & Nishiguchi, T. (2001). *Knowledge emergence – Social, technical, and evolutionary dimensions of knowledge creation.* New York: Oxford University Press.

Ottosson, S. (2010). *Frontline innovation management – Dynamic product & business development.* Stockholm: Ottosson & Partners.

Patton, M. Q. (2002). *Qualitative research & evaluation methods.* Beverly Hills, CA: Sage.

Pedersen, S. H. (2012). *Employee-driven innovation: A new approach.* Basingstoke: Palgrave Macmillan.

Røvik, K. A. (1998). *Moderne organisasjoner: trender i organisasjonstenkningen ved tusenårsskiftet.* Bergen-Sandviken: Fagbokforl.

Shook, J. (2008). *Managing to learn: Using A3 management process to solve problems.* Cambridge: Lean Enterprise Institute.

Smith, M., & Kleine, P. (1986). Qualitative research and evaluation: Triangulation and multimethods reconsidered. In D. Williams (Ed.), *Naturalistic evaluation (New directions for program evaluation).* San Francisco: Jossey-Bass.

Sobek, D. K., & Smalley, A. (2008). *Understanding A3 thinking: A critical component of Toyota's PDCA management system.* New York: Productivity Press.

Tashakkori, A., & Teddlie, C. (2010). *SAGE handbook of mixed methods in social & behavioral research.* Thousand Oaks, CA: Sage.

Womack, J. P., Jones, D. T., & Roos, D. (1990). *The machine that changed the world: Based on the Massachusetts Institute of Technology 5-million dollar 5-year study on the future of the automobile.* New York: Rawson Associates.

Yeasmin, S., & Rahman, K. F. (2012). 'Triangulation' research method as the tool of social science research. *BUP Journal, 1*(1), 154–163.

CHAPTER 2

The Financial Crisis

Abstract This chapter explores the reasons why the Norwegian industry performed well during the financial crisis and we draw the general lessons that can be learned from this. The chapter relies on the results of an extensive survey investigating how the economic crisis resulted in increased efficiency and effectiveness in Norwegian manufacturing. It paves the way for the remainder of the book by asking how such positive results can emerge out of an external shock, a crisis. This chapter also discusses how to understand the findings from the Norwegian case in a global context. Interestingly, the first part of the survey was completed before the financial crisis, and the second in its aftermath, offering a unique before-after situation analysis of business perspectives.

The chapter highlights the extraordinary circumstances in which the companies were in when the financial crisis struck the Western world with devastating consequences. Here, the effects on the automotive industry and the case companies are described.

© The Author(s) 2018
H. Holtskog et al., *Learning Factories*, Palgrave Studies in
Democracy, Innovation, and Entrepreneurship for Growth,
https://doi.org/10.1007/978-3-319-41887-2_2

THE FINANCIAL CRISIS

The Bigger Picture

In 2008, the financial market in the USA collapsed and several important large actors went bankrupt, which had devastating effects for the automotive industry (see Fig. 2.1).

The entire industry went from turbulent times in 2007 and 2008 to a deep recession in 2009. The turbulence of 2007 and 2008 can be explained by the rapid expansion following the upturn of 2004 to 2006. In this positive period, the carmaker industry tried to capture the growing markets in the BRICS[1] (Freyssenet, 2009) by building new factories to serve these countries which dramatically increased production capacity to international

Economic barometer for the automotive industry
1992-2009

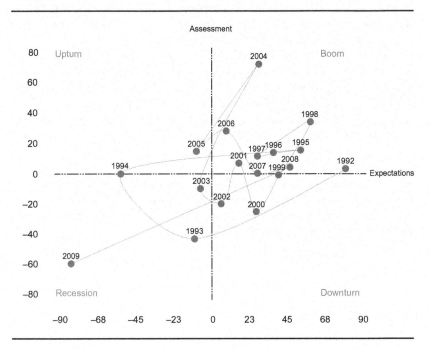

Fig. 2.1 Economic barometer
Source: IFO-Institute, 2010

surplus. As such, the turbulent times of 2007 and 2008 were financially constrained. As an example, Ford Motor Company restructured its operations and shut down some factories, as well as simplified the supplementary equipment offer for each car model. In late 2008 and 2009, the automotive industry went into a recession and carmakers went bankrupt, factories shut down, and the manufacture of new car models was postponed. General Motors and Chrysler needed government aid to stay in business. The previous boom or upturn period meant huge investments in a saturated global market, accompanied by increasing debt which made the industry vulnerable. Thus, we can consider these parameters as two major crises that hit the industry at roughly the same time. Some background to the Norwegian model can be informative before discussing how the crisis affected regional industry at Raufoss.

The Norwegian Model

Beginning in the 1950s and 1960s, researchers started to look into working conditions, power distributions, and work-life participation in Norwegian industry.[2] This research has since been categorized into five time phases up to the 2000s (Johnsen, 2012). The first phase was inspired by the human relations movement, focusing on individual motivation and self-realization. The second and third phases emphasized the broad democratic discussion in work-life and organizations. The focus here was initially on collective participation through indirect democracy, and later on direct democracy in the form of elected representatives from the workforce within the boards of directors. These two phases legitimized the security, stability, and workers' collective participation and joint actions, formalized in the Working Environment Act of 1977. The fourth phase tried to create mutual understanding for organizational development where the focal point was the organization as a discursive system that embodied collective understanding and discursively developed strategies. Finally, the fifth phase focused on the regionalization and networking of companies located in the same areas.

The Nordic countries' better management of the financial crises was the topic of the World Economic Forum in Davos 2011 (Dahl, 2011; Johnsen & Pålshaugen, 2011). According to the Organisation for Economic Co-operation and Development (OECD) calculations, Norway should not have been doing so well due to a large public sector, high taxes, and low spending on Research and Development (R&D). Different explanations were therefore offered such as the solidary wage policy, where low productive work has been replaced with high productive work (for instance, through the automatization of industry processes). That is, people working in high productive work with relative low wages for such. 'Terms of trade' provided another explanation as Norway sells high priced products and raw materials. Finally, the welfare state was brought forward, arguing that welfare services help companies with social costs, such as sick leave and temporary layoffs. In this last explanation, the small power distance, high trust levels, participatory goals, and strategy setting within companies are included. These explanations can be traced back to the different phases the Norwegian model has gone through, summarized in social partnership between worker (and workers' unions), owner (and the national owner's confederation called Næringslivets Hovedorganisasjon (NHO)), and the government (through the welfare state).

The Crisis at Raufoss Industrial Park[3]

This section seeks to explore the dynamic product development capabilities in the industrial cluster during the global downturn from 2008 to 2010. The results presented here are part of two different papers arguing that measuring dynamic capabilities such as product development, according to strategic capability analysis, does not give satisfactory answers. But, in this section, the results of the two studies are used to provide a deeper understanding of the extraordinary times in which this book investigated the companies. Note that only the most R&D-intensive companies and industries are investigated, as outlined in Table 2.1. The product column indicates what kind of business each company is involved in, coupled with the industry column that gives an indication of where in the value chain the company fits.

Most of the companies are internationally owned and therefore may have different pressures to cut costs than nationally owned ones. The international financial crisis hit the global marketplace, but some countries were hit harder than others. As such, an international enterprise will have different ways to save costs and different priorities than a national company. Being on the outskirts of Europe, cost savings in the Norwegian companies may be considered easier than in central European companies as the media and political attention of a closure or downscale would be less. There are no Original Equipment Manufacturers (OEMs) in the automotive industry and these companies are suppliers in the first or second tier. The defense company (C2) has some products that qualify the company to be an OEM; however, it is not a broad market and is governed by different rules unlike the car market.

From 2008 to 2010, the seven manufacturers downsized the number of employees from 2107 to 1655, a reduction of about 21 percent. As

Table 2.1 Description of companies (C) and research institutions (R) included in this study

Companies and R&D institutions	Industry	Ownership	Number of employees in 2010	Main products
C1	Water and gas distribution	International	49	Couplings, fittings, and adapters
C2	Defense and aerospace	Norwegian and Nordic	654	Medium and large caliber ammunition and missile products
C3	Automotive	International	716	Crash management systems
C4	Automotive	Norwegian	280	Air brake couplings
C5	Automotive	International	205	Exterior plastic components
C6	Automotive	International	113	Front and rear control arms
C7	Automotive	International	90	Steering columns
R1	Research and consulting	Industry and national research institutes	80	R&D
R2	Research and education	Public	270	R&D

seen from Fig. 2.2, only two companies have maintained or increased the number of employees during this period, while the remaining—automotive suppliers—suffered more than a 33 percent workforce reduction. When summarizing the R&D Human Resource Index,[4] which represents the cognitive background of firms' knowledgeable skilled workers, the number of employees has dropped from 172 to 114 (34 percent) for all seven companies. This is a considerable cut as a whole, and devastating in the long run due to the assumption that higher education equates higher economic returns (Giuliani & Bell, 2005). The index for two companies (**C3** and **C5**) significantly decreased. Reasons for this dramatic reduction of knowledgeable workers are twofold: first, they had to adjust capacity in accordance to reduced sales volume and, second, both firms faced major restructuring in the form of the holding company's bankruptcy (**C5**) and

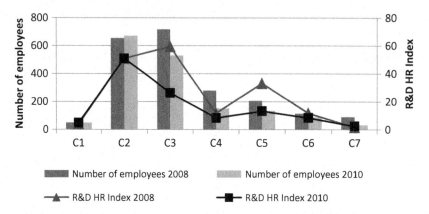

Fig. 2.2   Number of employees and R&D Human Resource Index

takeover (from a nationally owned to internationally owned company, **C3**) during the crisis. These events impacted greatly not only on the R&D departments but also on the cluster as a whole due to company size and R&D effort.

To investigate the manufacturers' ability to justify and exploit new information, questions were asked regarding changes in the customer base, product and project portfolio, participation in external R&D projects, and patents. These are indicators of knowledge creation efforts in the companies, which involve collaboration with a broad range of actors, for instance, suppliers, customers, R&D partners, investors, funding partners, and so on.

Figure 2.3 shows that, in total, the customer base for all seven companies increased by 17.5 percent from 2008 to 2010, where positive signs can be reported for five of them, and status quo for the remainder. Surprisingly, the automotive suppliers contributed the most to the increased customer base. Despite market turbulence and downsizing processes, they managed to develop new concepts and products, convincing new customers. This trend is also reflected in changes to each firm's product base, where all added products to their portfolios in the same period. An overall growth of eight percent in the number of unique products manufactured by the seven companies is registered. However, when looking at **C5** and **C3** there are indications of a threshold for how much activity that can be maintained with regard to new customer projects and product development as well as

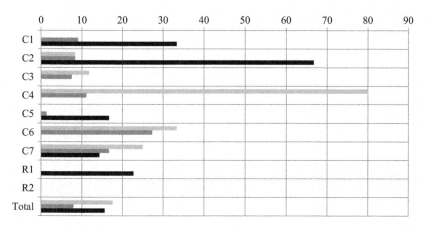

Changes in customer base (main products) from 2008 to 2010 [%]

Changes in product base from 2008 to 2010 [%]

Changes in number of R&D projects from 2008 to 2010 [%]

Fig. 2.3   Changes in customer, product, and R&D project base at firm level

the degree of downsizing of technical personnel. These two companies are at the lower end of the scale when it comes to adding new customers, projects, and products to their existing bases.

Participation in external R&D projects is regarded as an investment in ideas that the firm can then capitalize on. This implies creating new knowledge together with partners showing interest in the same ideas. Thus, such projects are considered important arenas for companies to invest time and money into long-term partnerships that can bring new insight and knowledge to keep up with—or even lead—technology development within strategic areas. Figure 2.3 presents changes in the number of R&D projects, which includes government-funded research projects and programs, together with local network arenas from 2008 to 2010, where the main trend is positive in the sense that the total number of R&D projects increased by 14 percent. Especially, C1 and C2 increased their R&D activity—the same companies that maintained their R&D Human Resource Indexes during the same period.

The last indicator defined is the number of patents to establish if there were any trends during the crisis. All companies report that they have ambitions to

Table 2.2   New patents since 2008

Company	C1	C2	C3	C4	C5	C6	C7	Total
Number of new patents since 2008	1	1	4	1	0	0	1	8

patent more than they used to but it is a costly, time-consuming process that involves anything from describing what is unique to claiming patent rights for a product, process, or concept. The interviewees could not tell exactly how many patents their company held at the outset of the crisis, but could report how many had been registered since 2008. This is presented in Table 2.2.

Table 2.2 shows that the manufacturers registered eight patents during the two years, but it is difficult to say if this number is high or low without having anything to compare it against. However, on a general basis, the companies claim that ever-increasing customer requirements in global demanding markets force them to rapidly develop new product- and process technologies. In that way, patenting does not make so much sense for protecting business concepts. Such policies may contribute to what is defined as the 'Norwegian puzzle' by the OECD (2007), where Norway is rated low on innovation indicators such as R&D intensity, patent number, high-tech jobs, and innovation rate, though Norwegian industry is considered productive, profitable, and competitive (even without the oil and gas sector).[5]

Intra-cluster Knowledge System

The first indicator—infrastructure collaboration—intends to capture the degree actors see the industrial park—Raufoss—as important to maintain and further develop a dynamic and competitive cluster. It is assumed that if the actors do not value co-localization and collaboration at the most basic level, it will negatively influence the higher levels of collaboration, that is, contributing and expecting access to common knowledge stocks. Several of the interviewees emphasized what they call the 'strategic park forum' as an important area for top managers to discuss infrastructure issues (rent, maintenance, access, environment, etc.). Further, the largest companies—C2, C3, and C5—point to the importance of preserving the cluster's critical mass, optimizing the conditions for both existing and new businesses. C2 also claims that the collaboration climate in this forum was never better than during the crisis. Whether this improved cooperation is owed to an extraordinary effort during crisis time or the fact that four out of the seven companies have changed CEO during those years is hard to tell. But, management priority is of course a prerequisite for creating a dynamic and vital strategic park forum.

Another indicator of intra-cluster knowledge development regards joint network and R&D efforts. There has been a national attempt to promote innovation in regional Norwegian clusters to provide long-term support with growth potential. The extended Raufoss regional cluster is among the 12 clusters in Norway that have been appointed this status. One of the main goals of this program is to develop new products, processes, and services from the competence network related to lightweight materials and automation. Another goal is developing an integration between industry, research institutions, universities, and the regional public sector. The supplies of knowledge-intensive products to globally demanding customers, together with the close collaboration between industry, universities, and local R&D institutions, have resulted in numerous research projects. In 2008, there was a total of 25 externally funded R&D projects reported, where at least two of the seven explored companies, in addition to the local R&D institutions $R1$ and $R2$, participated. In 2010, this number increased by 32 percent to 33 projects—a considerable growth which can be partly explained by the well-adapted calls from the Norwegian Research council as well as well-suited industrial projects. This is reflected in Fig. 2.4.

On the other hand, the number of R&D linkages, which indicates cluster commonness of the initiated R&D projects, shows a slight decrease by three percent. As illustrated, $C3$ and $C6$ reduced the number of linkages from 2008 to 2010, although the number of projects was maintained (respectively 12 and 9). The main reason for the decrease is therefore a change in the R&D projects' portfolio, from network projects to more specific R&D ones. $C3$, formerly Norwegian owned, also turned its attention to centralized R&D resources and projects within the $C3$ group (German-based company with more than 23,000 employees). On the contrary, $C2$, in accordance with its strategy, became more involved in R&D activities together with other cluster companies. Overall, the number of projects increased from four to seven and number of linkages increased by 15 percent over the period. The intra-cluster R&D indicator seems to remain strong during the crisis, but it is important to have in mind that R&D involves long-term projects which may not be affected in the short run.

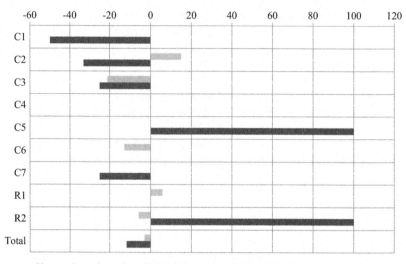

Changes in total number of R&D linkages from 2008 to 2010 [%]

Changes in total number of internal customer/supplier linkages from 2008 to 2010 [%]

Fig. 2.4   Changes in number of R&D and internal customer/supplier linkages

The third indicator, customer and supplier linkages, reflects the level of business between the companies in the cluster, including products and services. Examples of products are extruded profiles, cast aluminum, tools and components, and services (laboratory, testing, and validation). This indicator shows a degree of intra-cluster dependency to directly impact and improve one another's products and services. Figure 2.4 indicates that the number of intra-cluster customer and supplier linkages has decreased by almost 12 percent from 2008 to 2010. However, it turned out that this reduction was caused by minor changes in the firms' supplier bases (i.e., **C1, C2, C3**, and **C7**).

The fourth indicator measures the degree spillover effects that are influenced by the crisis. Spillover effects are agreed upon knowledge flows between companies to strengthen the cluster as a whole. This tacit agreement is something that originates from the fact that these companies share a common history and are located closely together. More concretely, employees' transfer from one company to another (either by lending agreements or by changing jobs) researchers and consultants working that bring knowledge with them inside the geographic area (Caniëls, 1999;

Ho & Verspagen, 2006). From economy geography theory, such spillover effects can explain why innovations seem to be concentrated in specific geographical areas, or Regional Innovation Systems (Braczyk, Cook, & Heidenreich, 2004; Niosi, 2012). The main interest here is to investigate whether local stocks of contextualized complex knowledge are not only accessible but also eventually absorbed by localized firms. Spillover effects can be found in various configurations, for instance: (a) direct support between companies; (b) use of local research institutions; and (c) new product and process ideas. From the interviews, there have been a few examples extracted that support these effects such as direct support and use of local R&D institutions and new possible ideas during the crisis. The local innovation system in terms of new products, processes, and services seems, however, to be exclusively driven by demanding customers. From this study, there is little evidence of spillover effects beside friendly support and cooperation in long-term R&D projects.

Moderators
From the indicators and results presented above, the impact of the crisis was not as evident as anticipated regarding efficient accumulation and adaption of knowledge. Despite the dramatic reduction in the number of employees and R&D human resource index, there are still considerable activities in attracting new customers, developing new products, participating in R&D projects, and patenting of new solutions. When looking at the category intra-cluster knowledge communication patterns, the results show a slight decrease in the number of intra-cluster linkages during the crisis, but, in general, companies seem to have some focus on helping each other to strengthen the cluster. However, the main priority is internal for each company. Thus, at first glance, the reduction in an organization's ability to acquire information does not give the impression of reduced capability to create knowledge and adapt it into new products. The same seems true for the ability to maintain relations and accumulate knowledge at cluster level, supporting the 'likelihood of survival' when embedded in an alliance (Gulati, 2007).

In this research, some moderators have been touched upon. Moderators are anticipated, in most cases, to positively affect output in the short run and can be seen either as intentional actions taken by the firms or as more accidental events. This means that dynamic capability must also be discussed in the terms of a set of moderators in addition to an instrumental way. Thus, the impacts of the crisis will be observable in a longer time lag than measured in this analysis. The lack of instantaneous impacts of the crisis upon dynamic capability can be attributed to the moderators which will now be explored.

Level of preparedness implies that an organization prior to the crisis had cut fixed costs to a minimum, as well as had implemented efficient Lean processes throughout the enterprise and introduced extremely professional information acquiring systems to adapt to customer requirements (Womack, Jones, & Roos, 1990). This attitude, together with the squeezed market, may have absorbed some of the shock created by the widespread substantial crisis. However, it is assumed that a thin line exists between reducing information to a minimum and missing crucial information which in turn may harm product functionality, reliability, and quality.

The increase in the number of new customers and products may have resulted from work done prior to the crisis. Capturing new customers and retaining existing ones in aerospace and automotive industries often involves long qualifying processes. Consequently, these processes will have materialized into contracts at the outset of, or even during, the crisis, thus, keeping the companies busy. This can be regarded as short-term trade-offs and may explain a great deal of the paradox observed in the increase in project number and stable cluster activity, alongside R&D staff reduction. However, the long-term effects of reducing market and development efforts might entail missed customers and contracts, indicating that the crisis will affect the businesses for many years to come. Nevertheless, as the EU introduced new regulations proposing that all cars registered from 2015 have to comply to a limit curve which states that the fleet average of 130 grams CO_2 per kilometer (ECE, 2010), the regional cluster at Raufoss had—and still has—many opportunities. Specifically, the cluster has over four decades of accumulated knowledge on lightweight solutions, mainly aluminum, part of the solutions to reduce vehicle weight. Hence, the car manufacturers' positioning may have positively affected product and customer bases in the cluster to meet the new regulations upon their implementation which affects its long-term success likelihood. This is further maintained by product development activity during the crisis regarding a degree of innovation whereby the possibility that projects initiated then require both less resources and comply more to a continuous innovation pathway than previous ones.

Another explanatory factor regards how companies make structural changes when faced with major volume drops. Traditionally, work experience and the number of years employed in the same organization have been fundamental principles in Norwegian working life for downsizing decision-making. This is not an unconditional principle, but is constituted in most employee and employer organizations' agreements because of the democratic debate and broad participation phases in the development of the Norwegian model. Assuming this principle is complied with, it is also probable that the most experienced personnel who hold most of the links to suppliers, customers, and R&D institutions are preferred over the younger and/or less experienced. Thus, the companies preserve several external links that are valuable in searching for new and relevant information. In addition, the companies appear to have a time horizon for planning and evaluating profitability that exceeds the one fiscal year model.

Further, dynamic capability as the level of externally funded research projects also acted as a moderator during the crisis phase. Such projects, mainly government funded, are often estimated to last for three to five years. Thus, having an appropriate product and technology portfolio at the onset of the crisis made competing in the market place easier. They managed to maintain—or improved—during the crisis with long-term research activities. Several of the companies considered the research project portfolio to be at a proper level in 2008 and managed to increase it in the successive two years. Overall, the discussion demonstrates that explaining dynamic capability in light of a financial crisis needs to consider a set of moderators.

CONCLUSION

This chapter presented the cluster's history in which the two companies (C3 and C6) are part of. Furthermore, it aimed to provide a deeper understanding of the crisis and the extraordinary times that occurred at the time of writing this book. Before going into the theory and data that represent the backbone of the thesis, the next chapter outlines the methodology. Thereafter, detailed case studies support the central argument of the benefit of social partnership at different societal levels.

NOTES

1. BRICS stands for Brazil, Russia, India, China, and South Africa.
2. Many ideas have come from Sweden and Denmark, but we concentrate on Norway.
3. This is taken from the results of a paper presented at the ISPIM conference in Canada and supported with a paper presented at ICED-09 at Stanford (Ringen & Holtskog, 2009; Ringen, Holtskog, & Endrerud, 2009).

4. This index is based on the following formula: R&D Human Resource
Index = 0.80 × Number of degrees + 0.05 × Master degrees + 0.15 × PhD.
5. Look back at the Norwegian model.

REFERENCES

Braczyk, H.-J., Cook, A., & Heidenreich, M. (Eds.). (2004). *Regional innovation system: The role of governances in a globalized world.* London: Routledge.
Caniëls, M. (1999). *Regional growth differentials.* PhD, Maastricht University.
Dahl, C. F. (2011). Stoltenberg selger 'nordisk modell' i Davos. *Aftenposten.* Retrieved from http://www.aftenposten.no/okonomi/innland/article4010273. ece#.UdriV234V8E
ECE. (2010). *EU energy in figures 2010, CO_2 emissions from transport by mode.* Directorate-General for Energy and Transport (DG TREN).
Freyssenet, M. (2009). *The second automobile revolution – Trajectories of the world carmakers in the 21st century.* New York: Palgrave Macmillan.
Giuliani, E., & Bell, M. (2005). The micro-determinants of meso-level learning and innovation: Evidence from a Chilean wine cluster. *Research Policy, 34,* 47–68.
Gulati, R. (2007). *Managing network resources: Alliances, affiliations, and other relational assets.* New York: Oxford University Press.
Ho, M. H. C., & Verspagen, B. (2006). The role of national borders and regions in knowledge flows. In E. Lorenz & B. Å. Lundvall (Eds.), *How Europe's econo-mies learn: Coordinating competing models* (pp. 50–79). Oxford: Oxford University Press.
IFO-Institute. (2010). *Annual report 2009.* Munich: Verband der Automobilindustrie.
Johnsen, H. (Ed.). (2012). *A collaborative economic model – The case of Norway.* Farnham: Gower.
Johnsen, H. C. G., & Pålshaugen, E. (2011). *Hva er innovasjon? Perspektiver i Norsk innovasjonsforskning bind 1.* Kristiansand: Høyskoleforlaget.
Niosi, J. (2012). *Building national and regional innovation systems: Institutions for economic development.* New York: Edward Elgar Publishing.
OECD. (2007). *OECD territorial reviews Norway.* Paris: Organisation for Economic Cooperation and Development.
Ringen, G., & Holtskog, H. (2009). *Product development in the financial crisis.* Paper presented at the ICED, Stanford University, USA.
Ringen, G., Holtskog, H., & Endrerud, J. O. (2009). *How the automotive and financial crisis affect innovations in an industrial cluster?* Paper presented at the 3rd ISPIM Innovation Symposium, Quebec City, Canada.

CHAPTER 3

Development of Suspension Parts Project

Abstract From a macro and national perspective, this chapter focuses on the specificities of a manufacturing sector, that is, the Norwegian automotive industry. The chapter introduces the reader to product development in the industry, demonstrating how the organization learns (or not) from the one product development project to the next. This descriptive approach as to how product development occurs in real settings is in stark contrast to the one presented in the firms' formal description of quality management systems and other types of formal displays. This chapter provides therefore, a unique insight in a) the discrepancies between firms' fragmented and not always coinciding representations of realities of real production processes and b) the challenges firms' meet in accumulating knowledge and know-how between projects.

INTRODUCTION

In this chapter, we provide data of the actual usage of a multi-dimensional framework, starting with organizational learning. This section begins with introductory investigations made by the research team that uncovered differences between espoused theory and theory-in-use. The automotive industry, however, is governed by strict procedures, quality standards, management systems, and so on that give the impression that the espoused theory describes how things are actually done. Finding that it is not true is

© The Author(s) 2018   37
H. Holtskog et al., *Learning Factories*, Palgrave Studies in
Democracy, Innovation, and Entrepreneurship for Growth,
https://doi.org/10.1007/978-3-319-41887-2_3

therefore surprising, and the investigation shows that a quality system is used, but not as a living, continually updated system with forms and schemas that describe the actual work done. Furthermore, these systems are not used for learning proposes. Learning is a face-to-face phenomenon, rather than reading what has been achieved in accordance to a system. Hence, this raises the classical distinction between informal and formal organizations, or fantasy versus real systems. However, this dualism will not provide more insight. Two different systems and organizations are interconnected and consist of interdependent parts that need to be accordingly analyzed. The analysis shows that people can work even if they do not agree on things, and that managers can maintain the organization by supporting effective and efficient work under circumstances of disagreement, acting as the linchpin. Overall, the chapter indicates the importance of organizational culture and facilitative management. It provides deeper insight into the learning model and defensive actions through the FMEA story. Specifically, the research group tried to sort out some of these actions in a workshop as the starting point in the effort to transform model O-I to model O-II learning. The chapter provides insight into how other tools and methods aimed to create a learning arena inside one particular project.

Organizational Learning

This section looks at the development of a suspension part for a North-European car manufacturer through the lens of organizational learning theory. In product-development projects, especially in the automotive industry, there are strict and complicated procedures to follow, standards that the company must be certified, customer quality systems that represent the customer demands, and structured project management systems. The company transforms and translates these external systems, procedures, and standards into its own equivalents. In this way, it represents the agreed upon procedures for decision-making and delegate one individual as the leader. The project team can be thought of as a boundary between the company collective and the rest of the organization or world. All in all, product-development project teams satisfy the basic conditions for becoming an organization as set by Argyris and Schön (1996, p. 8).

Throughout this book, the systems, implementation of standards, and procedures are representatives of knowledge embedded in routines and practices. In addition, any doubt of these systems along with experience can trigger changes that lead to learning both on individual and on organizational levels. To investigate learning and change, one method dominates relating to 'inferences of causal connections between action and outcomes and their implication for future action ...' (Argyris & Schön, 1996, p. 17) which uncovers the theory-in-use in the organization, both for former and for ongoing projects. However, other methods are also used to gain a clear picture of phenomena, espoused theory, and theory-in-use.

Difference Between Espoused Theory and Theory-in-Use

Espoused theory deals with how things should be or claim to be done, often represented in flow charts or procedures in different systems. Theory-in-use, on the other hand, describes how things are actually done. Ideally, these two 'theories' should be the same, but they are often not. However, many researchers provide theories as if this is the case.

Quality management theory and practices are arguably in such a category. Strong beliefs in forms and checklists are thought to bring espoused theory and theory-in-use together as one. Integrating specific project management tools, certification (revised annually) according to standards, and revision points are elements created to enforce and control that the two are the same. Yet, one must seriously question: *Is this true?* In the automotive industry, the quality regime is strict and has all these enforcing elements. While working with these companies, it was interesting to look deeper into this quality claim. If it *is* true, then the systems, tools, certification, and revision points will impact on how industry learns and creates knowledge. To investigate this claim, data from a survey are used. Nineteen companies partook, with 123 participants answering 81 questions, out of a total of 150 individuals targeted. All participants were working either directly or very closely with product development in the automotive industry. The results of the survey were presented at a workshop arranged for C6, which will be later returned to.

As C6 was interested in learning from past projects, we wanted to test how easy or accessible the documented experiences were from previous projects. C6 seemed to score above average for the industry at over 45 percent, which demonstrated that it was relatively easy to find previous experience (the industry average was 32 percent with a similar normal distribution). Nevertheless, this was somewhat of a surprise as the industry is quality aware and places huge efforts on quality systems and so on. Documentation is essential for the foundation of quality thinking. One can claim that the fundamental thought of being able to document all knowledge is embedded in the quality system; if it is not well documented, quality will suffer. Questioning this foundation, we asked how

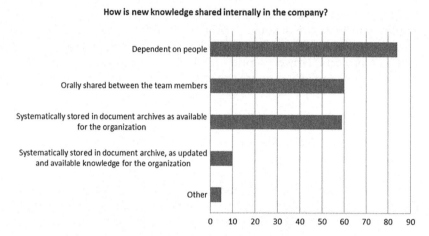

Fig. 3.1 Knowledge sharing

new knowledge is internally shared. Here, the respondents received five statements that they needed to value on a Likert scale, ranging from 1 to 5. The findings are represented in Fig. 3.1.

As indicated, knowledge sharing depends on those involved. Rules and standards for documentation, however, should eliminate such differences. In organizations within the automotive industry, this is rather surprising because of the huge amount of literature available on standardized work descriptions and the Lean tradition (Fujimoto, 1997, 1999; Liker, 2004; Morgan & Liker, 2006; Ohno, 1978; Shimokawa & Fujimoto, 2010; Taylor, 1911) which try to come up with one way of doing things to make it easier for learning purposes as well as consistency. Although, such a standardized work description should change regularly (Shimokawa & Fujimoto, 2010) for continuous improvement. Thus, standardization is the way of doing something that a group or organization has agreed to and should not depend on groups or individuals. We found that this was not something special to C6, but was in accordance with the industry average. Moreover, the figure shows that information is shared orally which we found unsurprising as flat and small organizational forms dominate Norwegian companies. Although, the paradox here relates to engineers' passion for standardization and explicit documentation on the one side, and oral sharing without documentation on the other.

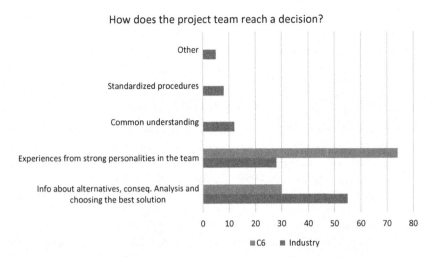

Fig. 3.2 Team decision-making

Decision-Making

Looking at engineering and the automotive industry from a distance, they seem to be very well organized and rational thinking dominates. Decisions are made based on information about alternative options, results from consequence analyses, and so on. These rationales are then set up against the goals for the project or organization. By doing things with broad participation, Lean tradition learning is promoted which is the reason why we wanted to assess how project teams reach decisions (see Fig. 3.2).

Answers to these questions came as somewhat of a surprise to us, as decisions seemed to be based on the experiences from strong personalities in the team, and not the rational choice of information about the alternatives, consequence analysis, and so on. Looking at the background of the people working in product development at C6, they all have high formal educations and long experiences in the automotive industry. As the decisions were not taken from a rational, common understanding or standardized procedures, the natural question became whether a high formal education and long experience inhibited learning.

To conclude, it seems that there are differences between espoused theory and theory-in-use even in the quality-loving automotive industry. However, establishing this claim does not bring us closer to understanding why there is a difference or what causes it. Specifically, is it the way the system is constructed that leads people to have different routines? Or, is it that having too many tools and procedures becomes impractical to follow?

Living Standardized Processes

Today, quality thinking is criticized for its focus on tools and red tape (Andersen, 1999; Brennan, 2001; Dahlgaard, Kristensen, Kanji, Juhl, & Sohal, 1998; Gotzamani & Tsiotras, 2001; Harry & Schroeder, 2000; Ho, 1995; Kiella & Golhar, 1997; Oakland, 2003; Powell, 1995; Taguchi & Clausing, 1990) resulting in little focus on the support role of daily work. The claim in this critique is that tools and forms are merely produced because the system demands them. We wanted to investigate how the formal processes set by the quality system work, and how they contribute to continuous improvement as there are no doubts that quality systems are important and play significant roles in value generation, particularly in product development (Cooper, 1993; Pyzdek & Keller, 2010; Taguchi, Elsayed, & Hsiang, 1989; Womack, Jones, & Roos, 1990). Thus, it led us to ask: How do the people working in product development at C6 think about the quality system? This is represented in Fig. 3.3.

People believe that they follow the routines set by the quality system, but interestingly, they experience that others are not following the routines

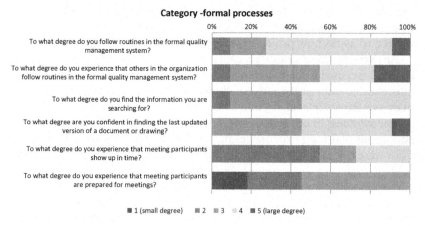

Fig. 3.3 Quality system formal processes

as well as themselves. It is therefore sometimes difficult to find the right information, although when they find it, they are confident that it is the latest version. This has to do with the timestamps on the files that date the forms. C6 has a documentation system that maintains order, but it also has a share disk volume where temporary files or working files are stored, which can sometimes be confusing. The last two points of Fig. 3.3 also tell us about an informal organization with a few people who have a lot of work to do. Here, C6 did not score significantly different than the rest of the industry.

The word 'living' indicates that improvements are continuously within the quality system, at the very heart of Lean (Liker, 2004; Liker & Hoseus, 2008; Womack et al., 1990). However, we wanted to understand how continuous improvement may look in the product-development department, and not just in the production line which is in focus in the Lean tradition (Womack & Jones, 1996). Figure 3.4 illustrates our findings.

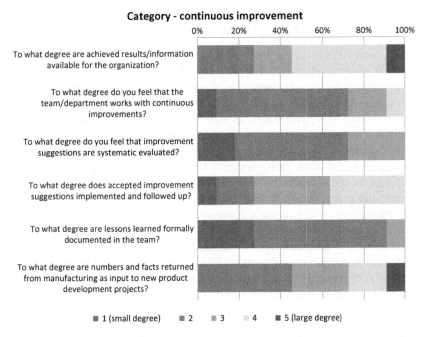

Fig. 3.4 Continuous improvement of quality system

The R&D department feels that results and information should be available to the rest of the organization, though this department does not work much on improving its own work habits. At first, this can look a little strange. The company competes in a very competitive global industry; therefore, we suspected a strong focus on continuous improvement. When asked, the R&D department tends to think in different terms. Everything it does is about improvement, and making the product the best it can at that specific time. This is the nature of product development, and its members do not think of it as continuous improvement. For them, continuous improvement is about setting up a project called 'continuous improvement' that would have the sole purpose of changing routines, forms, workflows, and so on. The workshop rectified this misunderstanding. Now, bringing the attention back to the last two questions in Fig. 3.4, it seems that the lessons learned were not formally documented, although were after a project had ended. Numbers and facts from production do not serve as important input to product-development projects, which is a point that C6 took very seriously, and later did much to improve.

Advanced Product Quality Planning: Checklists

Going back to the critique that too many tools make work impractical, the research team investigated how the checklists were filled out, using the insight to explore if the construction of systems is so complicated that people do not use them as intended. The team designated to C6 started by looking at the online document library, as well as the shared disks on the internal network for the documentation of recent projects. Our interest was to see if every document was completed, which standards and management systems are required, and when each document was created. A checklist is an important tool in the Advanced Product Quality Planning (APQP) method to ensure that every essential element is done at a specific phase. These checklists are audited by classification companies for ISO certification and important to customers regarding progress and performance. As such, checklists embrace one of the main types of official forms in a quality system and key to achieve and maintain different certifications as exemplified in Fig. 3.5.

Searching through the huge number of documents, we made some interesting discoveries. Starting with 209 projects at APQP 0 (the early phase of customer contact) and going through to APQP 3 (the development phase) with approximately 50 projects, the results were rather gloomy (Fig. 3.6).

Quality Assurance Plan

Production   ☐ Prototype ☐ Pre-Production ☐ Production

Part number	Part name		Document number
Project (name, no.)	Drawing number		Drawing issue
Responsible for the QAP	Date	Issue	Distribution

Activity	Resp.	Due Date	Approved	Comments
1. 1 Check of Input Data		12.12.2012		
2.1 2.1 Flow Chart				
2.2 2.2 P - FMEA				
2.3 2.3 Control plan				
3. 3.Checking Aids				
4. 4. MSA Studies				
5. 5. BoM and RTG Registration				
6. 6. Order Purchased Material				
7. 7. Purchased Material Approved				
8. 8. Tools				
9. 9. Production Equipment				
10. 10. Environment				
11. 11. Work Instruction				
12. 12. Rework Instruction				
13. 13. Inspection Instruction				
14. 14. Packaging Instruction				
15. 15. Maintenance Instruction				
16. 16. Visualisation of work area				
17. 17. Training				
18. 18. Run at Rate				
19. 19. Dimensional Results				
20. 20 . Test Results (PV)				
21. 21 .Capability Studies				
22. 22. Containment Plan				
23. 23. Process Approval				
24. Quality Assurance Report				
25. 25 .Customer Approval				
26.				
27.				
28.				
29.				
The QAP is performed and approved (Production Manager)		Date		

Fig. 3.5 Example checklist (borrowed from company C4)

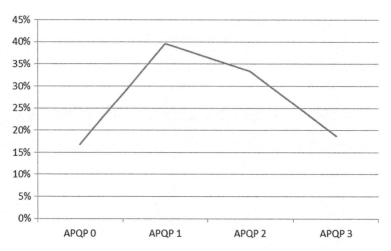

Fig. 3.6   Checklist completeness ratio

The APQP 0 checklist is for verifying the activities before an offer is given, while APQP 1, 2, and 3 are for the verification of activities in the phases from received orders at the start of series production. These checklists should be filled out by a cross-functional team, and serve as the bases for decisions before going on to the next stage (it can be argued that some activities overlap across the different stages, but this did not influence the findings). Some of the missing checklists were found on shared network volumes being used as a workplace with lots of subdirectories, or on the PC of the person responsible for a specific checklist. This meant that most lists were not available to the organization, as well as documented that the belief of the developers always working with the latest version was false. We discovered that some checklists were complete but stored on the PC of the person in charge of the project, meaning that they were not available to others. We also discovered that the time stamp on the files was just days ahead of the project audit. Looking at the underlying work that the checklist was supposed to document, we discovered that most of it was done—even though some of the work had already been completed—but in a different way than that described by the internal quality and management system. Such findings were interesting and made us look deeper into how the work, which was documented correctly, was conducted. Here, we found traces of the same—that is, individual procedures that differ from what is internally described as the 'correct way' that were later transformed into the 'correct way' for the official documentation. The next step was to investigate the consequences of such procedural deviations by investigating all the projects according to time, resources, cost, quality, and 'ramp-up' (scaling the project up for mass production). From this, we found no coherence between the missing or empty checklists and unprofitable projects. Importantly though, we found that the management system, which defined COP 1 and 2^1 as a marketing department activity, had in fact more activities related to the R&D department. Additionally, many decisions made here, in this early stage, impacted how the project developed, and the lack of R&D personnel here can have major consequences.

Overall, we documented a fragmented working method in the organization that was heavily influenced by the person in charge, thus making lessons learned across projects difficult due to the multiple way of doing things. Little efforts were made in developing the quality and management system for the routines and procedures, 'living' and according to theory-in-use. In addition, the quality manager was very eager to point out the 'correct way' of doing things. At the same time, every project manager we interviewed indicated the importance of having flexible and adaptable processes, claiming that the automobile manufacturers demanded such processes. This seemed to be contradictory: strong claims of 'one correct way' while being flexible and adaptable.

Conclusions of the Introductory Investigations

Within the automotive industry, product development is thought of as a strict and formal process with decision gates, quality systems, management systems, reports, customer demands, and change orders. Underneath these very strict and formal processes lies an informal, alternative way for everyday working life in the R&D department. Forms are not filled out for documentation during the work process, but rather as a necessity because of customer demands, and are often completed just ahead of the deadline for such a report. The work is satisfactorily achieved, though filling out the forms is more of a hassle. Learning from others is realized mostly informally through oral means. Indeed, there is a system of documentation that works, but developers do not seem to be involved with this. Instead, they prefer to communicate orally with each other. Experience is something that weighs heavy when decisions are made, along with having strong personalities. This finding stands in contrast to the rational system that the companies claim to have. Standardized processes are not 'living' or something that is continuously improved. Formal processes are more often followed when the time comes to report to the customer, while checklists are only done when necessary and not seen as helpful. There are significant differences between espoused theory and theory-in-use, and it is interesting to see what kind of theory-in-use is present in the organization. However, before doing this, some emerging questions are put forward.

The espoused theory and the theory-in-use show a difference between the formal and informal organization, or 'the fantasy and real systems.' However, these two cannot be analyzed separately as they are tightly interconnected, consisting of interdependent parts of the social system (Whyte, 1949). Seemingly, the formal systems are followed, but do not reflect the way the actual work is conducted (see Fig. 3.6). The organization seems to make decisions without agreeing on things (see Fig. 3.1). This raises a question: How do actors coordinate their work, if they do not agree? Moreover, how does a manager ensure the system does not fall apart? Figure 3.3 indicates an individualistic learning mode dominating the formal organizational learning. However, it can also indicate one key source of job satisfaction '... *in the interaction shaped by members of the work group*' (Roy, 1959), focusing on small groups developing into distinctive sub-cultures with social structures of statuses and roles. Finally, how do these sub-cultures deal with outside pressures when there are little or no substitutes for such high-qualified work in this community? These questions are central to the following chapters on organizational culture and facilitative management.

Defensive Actions and Learning Model O-I

This example refers to one of the case company's experience and use of Failure Mode and Effects Analysis (FMEA). FMEA can be defined as a tool intended to recognize and evaluate the potential failure of a product or process and the effects, and to identify actions to eliminate or reduce eventual potential failures and the documentation of the process (Ford-Motor-Company, 2004). This tool is normally described in quality standards, requiring automotive suppliers to be mainly certified according to the former QS 9000 and its APQP process, the detailed manual by the Automotive Industry Action Group (AIAG) and Toyota's Design Review Based on Failure Mode (DRBFM). Both case companies, C3 and C6 are certified according to ISO/TS16949 which aligns existing US, German, French, and Italian automotive quality system standards within the global automotive industry. It also specifies the quality system requirements for the design/development, production, installation, and servicing of automotive-related products.

The FMEA tool ends with a risk priority number (RPN):

$$RPN = Severity \times Occurrence \times Detection - for\ each\ failure\ mode\ detected.$$

- Severity is defined as the result of a failure effect on the function of a system perceived by the user;
- Occurrence defines the cause of a failure and its frequency probability; and
- Detection is how the appropriate suggested actions are tested.

If the RPN is higher than a predefined value, or the individual values exceed a set limit, action must be taken. The output from this tool is of course action plans to guide further problem-solving, but it also provides input to control plans, equipment investments, and manufacturing routines. By continuously updating FMEA with the experiences of testing and production, companies can use it as a common living database of learning. In addition, the tool is regarded by many QA managers[2] as one of the most important learning devices in the quality system.

The case company C6 has traditionally defined the use of FMEA within both products and processes in its product-development projects, in which the former is input to the PFMEA[3] process. Knowing that the company had launched four relatively similar products over the past eight years—known as carryover products—it was of interest to track its FMEAs for traces of explicit learning. By looking for similar failure mode statements in these eight FMEAs, as well as decreasing values of occurrence and detection by time, and therefore RPNs, it should be apparent whether there is evidence of learning. If failure modes detected in the first statement were excluded in the last FMEA, it is assumed that action has been taken and issues have been solved and therefore no longer regarded as critical. Surprisingly, many failure modes occurred with the same risk number values as in the previous FMEA (shown in Table 3.1) indicating either a copy–paste culture or status quo in continuous improvement work, or perhaps that they simply had forgotten what was previously improved on.

Table 3.1   Example of FMEA tracking

Product type					
Process	Failure mode	Product X1	Product X2	Product X3	Product X4
Incoming material	Faulty profile (surface)	Risk values 8/2/4—focus on supplier routines reduces risk values to 8/2/2	Risk values 8/2/4— requirements for surface quality established to reduce risk values to 8/2/2	Risk values 8/2/4— requirements for surface quality established to reduce risk values to 8/2/2	Risk values 7/2/1 after possible transport damages are taken care of by control cards

As the FMEAs demonstrated little evidence of continuously living documents, it was also interesting to look at what types of actions they suggested and what type of risk element they were directed toward. Many actions related to adding control mechanisms which were directed to detecting occurrence and rejecting eventual failures. This must be seen in the context of the FMEA, in which a group of people sits together outlining potential failure modes and risks. Everyone agrees that this proactive work is important, but spending time questioning the root cause[4]—concerning something that may or may not happen in the future—is often seen as less valuable than solving real problems detected internally or externally. Therefore, to save both costs and time in the short run, developers tended to add some sort of control to detect occurrences rather than solving its root cause. In addition, it demonstrates how the organization relies on skills to fight potential fires. Another reason why it most likely put effort into detection in order to reduce RPNs is the timing of the FMEA sessions. As emphasized by the case company and through observation, FMEAs are likely to be conducted later in a product-development project. By implication, it is therefore too late to impact previous decisions without major additional effort. This is probably why many failure modes are repeated over time in FMEAs. However, not all negative. In the FMEA process for the newest product, it was observed that personnel had used data from a previous project to analyze the problem. This is in accordance with the observed emerging focus on improvement of the use of FMEA as an efficient tool. As one respondent noted: '*we have to use it anyway, so why not use it as intended?*' Prior to this statement, the research group presented their findings in a workshop for leaders and workers in the development department.

The Workshop

The FMEA problem was a major topic at the workshop. Additionally, several interviews with those involved were conducted. After seeing the research teams' documentation, the CEO defined the problem by commenting that '*interaction between manufacturing and product development has to be improved. When a problem occurs in production, its potential negative effects and possible solutions should be documented in the FMEA, either as new input or as adjustments to existing failure modes.*' However, he did not address the underlying problem of single-loop learning and defensive actions. Arguments from the workshop and interviews included the following points:

- High-RPNs are normally incentives to act, but updating the FMEA after the implementation of specific actions is not common. Hence, the monitoring of initiatives could be improved to make the tool more active and dynamic. It was mentioned as an excuse for the common practice.
- In projects, potential and real problems are detected at many levels and in different contexts/phases both formally and informally. It is therefore difficult to integrate everything into the FMEA. Often, problems detected at an early project stage are more likely to be documented than failures in pre-serial production. Another excuse for the practice.
- Initial FMEAs are often copies of previous ones, as well as the failures. Consequently, the assumption that things are okay, or even better than they really are, is applied to new projects. Thus, the company can exhibit control of its environment, but in reality this is built on false premises. The starting point for turn of the debate.

These excuses sparked a debate that led to an honest expression of the suppressed feeling toward FMEA as listed:

1. FMEA sessions take too much time compared to their benefits. In relatively small organizations where individuals are engaged in many activities, it is difficult to gather a competent group and spend the time needed to conduct a reasonable FMEA.
2. The highly subjective meaning behind valuing a potential risk causes discussions at every FMEA session. Even though the same team is gathered frequently, the details and definitions are discussed every time, thus wasting 30–45 minutes of every meeting.
3. There is a tendency to involve too many people when arranging an FMEA session.

One interviewee said that *'in the pressure of daily work, it is difficult to find time to meet, and even if I do, someone else will not bother to attend. So, why bother spending time on these meetings?'* The second thing it indicates needs a bit explaining. The company is located in two buildings, one for production and one for development and administration. People working in one building would claim their colleagues competent, implying that those in the other building were not. Production workers were often absent because of stops in production and people saw it as an excuse for not attending. Alternatively, they laughed because FMEA done properly should have avoided such hindrances.

The second listed point above clearly states that reasons behind the RPN number were not based on facts and figures from the formal systems, but rather on something that annoys some person. Basing the discussion on such premises meant it dragged out and became increasingly uninteresting for the rest of the group, who would then not actively participate in the discussion. The third point is a consequence of the second. When losing such subjective, heated debates, the person would try to mobilize others of the same opinion to the next meeting. The leader of FMEA meetings was asked why he allowed this. His answer was somewhat confusing. First, he pointed to the CEO who wanted a broad and democratic discussion of these important issues. Second, he said that he had no power to say no to such requests: *'If you say yes one time to one individual you cannot say no to another.'*

Consequently, FMEA meetings were seen as something of a hassle, lengthy, pointing out subjective meanings, and ending with no good conclusions. A control undertaken by the research team compared one sub-production line that stated zero in the RPN of one FMEA in an ongoing product, with the average idle time for production. The goal set for this particular sub-production line was 80 percent idle. The real figure was under 50 percent and still there were no severe occurrences detected in the FMEA form. Asking the operators, they said that small stops were not registered into the systems: *'If you have 50 small stops in your shift; what is most important—to get things running or to make sure to type it into the system.'* This statement indicates how operators feel time pressure and do not fully understand the reason why recording stops is important. Confronted with a heated discussion from a former FMEA meeting, one of the operators told the researchers that he understood the importance. However, the choices in the reporting system never seem to fit the actual problems, making it challenging to use the system. Lack of training in system use was also mentioned, and finally, the action groups. An action group is a multidisciplinary group that is formed to look at crucial and pressing issues in production. Often senior employees from the development department (in the other building) led these groups. Some of the developers had good insight into production process, but not all of them. The operators felt inferior to these highly educated people and the situation was more like an interrogation than an investigation to find the root cause of problems whereby 'quick fixes' were the norm.

Efforts to Transform Model O-I to Model O-II

From these findings, the company outlined some action guidelines to improve FMEA performance. For example, the FMEA process was split into core-manufacturing processes, and every issue concerning equipment was separated into equipment FMEA. The entire product-development department obviously did not agree upon these changes; the opponents argued that when separating process and equipment, many important issues might be overlooked. The intention was to maintain the focus, while narrowing down the area of responsibility for each group. In the form itself, core-manufacturing processes were grouped together and inside each group, events were classified either as reoccurring or project specific. Reoccurring events were either an issue for a task group or something that could not be solved. Project specific events were focused in the meetings, backed up with data and information from the production or other systems. Grouping in this way made the process of discussion more easily focused. In addition, preparation before FMEA sessions, in the form of numbers and facts, would be encouraged. Discussions could then be more concrete and time efficient, instead of simply relying on intuition, individual judgment, and current issues. Finally, the FMEA process should be initiated earlier in projects, only then, can enough time be dedicated to root cause analyses.

Central Argument

These examples clearly show that it is easier taking action to solve real problems than focusing on preventing perceived ones. A mismatch between expected and obtained outcomes, whether detected by an internal test or customer, is more likely to be brought to people's attention than prioritizing subjective descriptions of possible future states. Therefore, triggered problem-solving by real events is less likely to be documented in FMEAs, indicating that detected failure modes, which score higher than acceptance criteria, can be defined as single-loop learning[5] (Argyris & Schön, 1996).

These failure modes tend to be treated by added control mechanisms instead of root cause analysis, and organizational learning and performance remain within the existing framework. However, some considerations or actions about potential future risks, whether categorized as single-loop learning or not, are probably better than ignorance, or a 'wait-and-see' attitude. However, as time is always a limitation the potential to further improve the facilitation of FMEA should be encouraged. Wasted time due to existing poor processes has an alternative cost, so the slight traces of Model I behavior[6] when trying to improve FMEA performance should be overcome and transferred into Model O-II actions. Such a transformation will certainly improve the product development process. As stated in Toyota's DRBFM,[7] a good discussion when making changes and risk concerns visible should be emphasized (Hirokazu & Hiroshi, 2005).

Implementation

From the above improvement suggestions, the development department together with the CEO decided to focus on a few key points that were regarded as both important and achievable for a busy organization facing the emerging global financial crisis. Creating a learning arena where highly visualized key project information can be viewed was also proposed as an overall structure to manage several other improvement suggestions. Inspired by Toyota's Obeya room ('large room' in Japanese), which is used to keep track of technical and financial key information, together with project timeliness and coordination (Liker, 2007), the research team wanted to create a learning arena dedicated to this purpose, with available wall space for placing important information. However, we had to settle with a whiteboard due to office limitations. To provide this valuable information 'room' for the engineers working on the projects, much effort was put into integrating existing tools and requirements. The starting point for this integration was the FMEA. It was agreed that an appropriately conducted FMEA should provide valuable input for:

- Issue lists (list of important things to do in the project);
- Control plans (summary of defect prevention and reactive detection techniques);

- Checklists (provide guidelines for new designs);
- Lessons learned (results from post-project reviews); and
- DFMEA (D = design) linkage to PFMEA (P = process) via a characteristics matrix.

The intention was that an unacceptable RPN from an FMEA should be reflected in the project issue list while requiring follow-up in the form of lessons learned. The latter had to be as simple as possible due to the claimed difficulties with expressing what has been learned in the written form. This is the reason why Toyota's A3 communication format, which visualizes data on a single sheet of paper and only leaves limited space for written explanations, was introduced as an alternative method. According to Liker (2007), three A3 formats take place: the status story, the info story, and the problem-solving story. The problem-solving story describes the outcome of the so-called LAMDA (Look, Ask, Model, Discuss, and Act) process, which is similar to the PDCA.[8] It provides a method of capturing lessons learned in an efficient way while agreeing actions should be followed up. Unfortunately, filtering and compressing thoughts onto a single sheet of paper where others have their questions answered is not necessarily straightforward. As noted by Kennedy (2003), the process of making an A3 calls for reflection and a deeper understanding of the problem at hand, or as stated by Liker (2007): '*It's much more about disciplined thinking than about any particular A3 writing technique.*' If the problem-solving process uncovers new knowledge for the company and provides acceptable RPN values, this knowledge should serve as input for checklists and control plans, as well as updated feedback to the FMEA. If not, a new problem-solving approach is needed. This reasoning is summarized as a process chart below, in addition to the more general information on the left side, illustrating the information board in the learning arena (Fig. 3.7). The flow figure on the right side shows the idealized learning arena. All high RPN values should be listed in the issue list and A3 form and used to find the core problem and an optimal solution to it.

After putting in place a method of implementation that aims at simplifying, visualizing, integrating, and documenting the product development process within an existing framework, the next step was to find a project where these new ideas could be experimented with. A newly started project to develop a front control arm for North European car manufacturer was chosen as a case; the project manager welcomed us researchers, and some new thoughts were ready to be implemented.

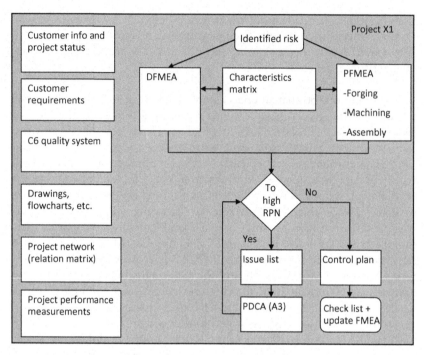

Fig. 3.7   Idealized learning arena C1

Results

The concept was outlined in December 2008 in conjunction with participation in project meetings to understand the new task which was introduced to the project team in January 2009. At the beginning, the focus was on streamlining the FMEA process and deciding upon interfaces between different FMEAs, particularly between processes and equipment, and the level of details and number of participants. This discussion continued until about June, when a template was proposed and implemented. For a long time, the FMEA process had been seen as cumbersome, so despite delayed progress in the learning arena, this was an important activity to accomplish before moving forward. Meanwhile, project meetings were held in the learning arena where the researchers continuously updated part of the information board. The project members frequently used the board to point out important information in discussions, although they showed little interest in contributing to—or maintaining—its information. This realization is fully in accordance with the argument by Morgan and Liker (2006) who note that tools at Toyota only work if it is the engineers themselves who contain the information, maintain it; only then is it credible enough so that others use the knowledge. Short briefs were held to teach the project members the basics behind how to conduct an A3, and in July 2009, the project manager showed us an A3 he had made to describe a problem-solving process. A required seal ability test, pointed to in the DFMEA, had discovered that the seal protecting the stud joint did not resist the necessary pressure before starting to leak. Seemingly, this could end here in a success story of transforming model O-I learning and defensive actions into model O-II learning. However, it would not give the 'correct' picture and leave out important aspects that are vital for outsiders when they try to learn from it.

Summary: Organizational Learning

This chapter shows that even in industries with strict formal systems, the espoused theory and theory-in-use differs. Defensive actions and learning model O-I were illustrated by the FMEA form procedure. Reoccurring failure and a copy–paste method demonstrated little evidence of continuously living formal documents. Endless discussions that often became sidetracked stood as examples of defensive actions. The FMEA example ended in describing efforts to transform model O-I to model O-II learning. In addition, it raised the awareness that FMEA forms were valuable input to other important documentations and the learning process as such. However, even a single-loop learning process is better than ignorance or a wait-and-see attitude. A mismatch between expected and obtained outcomes will trigger a problem-solving event. A real event is much better for root cause analysis and double-loop learning than FMEA's thought of detecting failure modes of future events.

This is not to say that formal systems of organization are not important. Formal systems give directions for learning by categorizing, focusing on the learning process, and creating a common 'language' for participants. However, the examples clearly show that formal systems do not capture the actual working procedures. In addition, the conclusion of these introductory investigations raises several important questions that the following chapters develop. First, the cultural aspects of the learning processes in the organization are discussed, setting the focus on the interconnected and interdependent parts of the social system. Moreover, informal coordination, job satisfaction, sub-cultures, statuses, roles, and dealing with the extraordinary circumstances during the financial crisis are explored.

NOTES

1. COP = customer-oriented processes.
2. In the case companies and in the rest of the industry at Raufoss.
3. Process FMEA (PFMEA)—how the risks regard the production processes (FMEA for products is called Design FMEA/DFMEA).
4. The root cause is the real problem and not the symptoms of a problem. There are many techniques to find the root cause, for example: 5 times why, PDCA, LAMDA, and so on.
5. The governing rules are operationalized rather than questioned.
6. Behavior that inhibit the questioning of governing rules.
7. DRBFM = Design Review Based on Failure Mode.
8. PDCA = Plan, Develop, Control, and Act. A method for finding the root cause of a problem and permanently solving it.

REFERENCES

Andersen, B. (1999). *Business process improvement toolbox.* Milwaukee: ASQ Quality Press.

Argyris, C., & Schön, D. (1996). *Organizational learning II: Theory, method, and practice.* Reading: Addison-Wesley Publishing Company.

Brennan, L. (2001). Total quality management in a research and development environment. *Integrated Manufacturing Systems, 12*(2), 94–102.

Cooper, R. (1993). *Winning at new products: Accelerating the process from idea to launch* (2nd ed.). Reading: Addison-Wesley Publishing Company.

Dahlgaard, J. J., Kristensen, K., Kanji, G. K., Juhl, H. J., & Sohal, A. S. (1998). Quality management practices: A comparative study between east and west. *International Journal of Quality & Reliability Management, 15*(8/9), 812–826.

Ford-Motor-Company. (2004). *FMEA handbook version 4.1.* Ford Design Institute.

Fujimoto, T. (1997). The dynamic aspect of product development capabilities: An international comparison in the automobile industry. In A. Goto & H. Odagiri (Eds.), *Innovation in Japan* (pp. 57–59). Oxford: Oxford University Press.

Fujimoto, T. (1999). *The evolution of a manufacturing system at Toyota.* New York: Oxford University Press.

Gotzamani, K. D., & Tsiotras, G. D. (2001). An empirical study of the ISO 9000 standard's contribution towards total quality management. *International Journal of Operations and Production Management, 21*(10), 1326–1342.

Harry, M. J., & Schroeder, R. (2000). *Six Sigma: The breakthrough management strategy revolutionizing the world's top corporations.* New York: Currency.

Hirokazu, S., & Hiroshi, N. (2005). Reliability problem prevention method for automotive components-development of GD'3' activity and DRBFM method for stimulating creativity and visualizing problems. *Transaction of Society of Automotive Engineers of Japan, 36*(4), 163–168.

Ho, S. K. M. (1995). Is the ISO 9000 series for total quality management. *International Journal of Physical Distribution & Logistics Management, 25*(1), 51–66.

Kennedy, M. N. (2003). *Product development for the Lean enterprise, why Toyota's system is four times more productive and how you can implement it.* Richmond: The Oaklea Press.

Kiella, M. L., & Golhar, D. Y. (1997). Total quality management in an R&D environment. *International Journal of Operations and Production Management, 17*(2), 184–198.

Liker, J. (2004). *The Toyota way: 14 management principles from the world's greatest manufacturer.* New York: McGraw-Hill.

Liker, J. (2007). *Tools & technology.* Presentation. Gardermoen, Oslo.

Liker, J., & Hoseus, M. (2008). *Toyota culture: The heart and soul of the Toyota way.* New York: McGraw-Hill.

Morgan, J., & Liker, J. K. (2006). *The Toyota product development system, integrating people, process and technology.* New York: Productivity Press.

Oakland, J. S. (2003). *Total quality management: Text with cases.* Amsterdam: Butterworth-Heinemann.

Ohno, T. (1978). *The Toyota production system.* Tokyo: Diamond.

Powell, T. C. (1995). Total quality management as competitive advantage: A review and empirical study. *Strategic Management Journal, 16*, 15–37.

Pyzdek, T., & Keller, P. A. (2010). *The Six Sigma handbook: A complete guide for green belts, black belts, and managers at all levels.* New York: McGraw-Hill.

Roy, D. F. (1959). Banana Time: Job satisfaction and informal interaction. *Human Organization, 18*, 158–168.

Shimokawa, K., & Fujimoto, T. (2010). *The birth of Lean.* Cambridge, MA: Lean Enterprise Institute.

Taguchi, G., & Clausing, D. (1990). Robust quality. *Harvard Business Review, 68*(1), 65–75.

Taguchi, G., Elsayed, E. A., & Hsiang, T. C. (1989). *Quality engineering in production systems.* New York: McGraw-Hill.

Taylor, F. W. (1911). *The principles of scientific management*. New York: Harper & Brothers.

Whyte, W. F. (1949). The social structure of the restaurant. *American Journal of Sociology, 54*, 302–310.

Womack, J. P., & Jones, D. T. (1996). *Lean thinking: Banish waste and create wealth in your corporation*. New York: Free Press.

Womack, J. P., Jones, D. T., & Roos, D. (1990). *The machine that changed the world: Based on the Massachusetts Institute of Technology 5-million dollar 5-year study on the future of the automobile*. New York: Rawson Associates.

CHAPTER 4

Organizational Culture: The Differentiated Perspective

Abstract This chapter scrutinizes the micro level of the industrial production processes, that is, the level of firm. It shows how global manufacturing/managerial trends, sectoral specific factors, national contexts, and firm specific features are represented into firms' observable cultural aspects and artifacts. The analysis provides the deeper understanding of subcultures and their respective behaviors, as well as, functions in a manufacturing context.

INTRODUCTION

Organizational culture as social glue, where common ideas, symbols, and values can be examples, is important for understanding the making of knowledge in an organization. However, it comes with important conditions of being able to 'speak the same language,' trust each other, and so on. The previous chapter questioned the notion of the 'right' picture. This section will bring some other ways of describing the foundations for knowledge making and learning in product-development projects by focusing on culture. This focus will start with the cohesive relationship between the Original Equipment Manufacturer (OEM) and supplier. It will be briefly put into the celebrated and Nobel Prize winning theory of Transaction Cost Economics (TCE), and in this way highlighting the hard and cold reality of business transactions and understanding of doing business in an integrated and global value chain.

© The Author(s) 2018
H. Holtskog et al., *Learning Factories*, Palgrave Studies in
Democracy, Innovation, and Entrepreneurship for Growth,
https://doi.org/10.1007/978-3-319-41887-2_4

Another theory is then introduced, the splitting theory, to deal with the analytical problem of defensive actions without saying people are stupid or mean. Splitting allows a manager to understand why people seem to behave irrationally and resist.

The focus then turns to the differentiated culture perspective by telling and analyzing different stories. The first story tells about a student group visit and highlights the notion of splitting. After this story the focus turns to war and hero stories starting out with comparing 'conventional industry,' that is, telling about the contradictory demands, constant threats of failing, and pressure. The third story is called the Easter action where difficulties with a suspension arm almost resulted in a very costly recall of the car model; in addition, there is a story about how one employee of C6 gained the hero status after finding faults in an Italian car manufacturer's assembly line. The story illustrates the abilities needed in a problem-solver in order to become a hero. The fourth story, Christmas action, deals with the new pole test when developing a new bumper for German sports car. The story adds a new dimension to the hero status and the proverb 'Crisis create heroes,' analyzing the spillover effects of the proverb into an understanding of the engineers or developers as craftsmen or artisans and the inconsistencies in the culture. Taken together, these points highlight an understanding that accountability-based quality control does not produce quality.

VALUE CHAIN RELATIONSHIP IN TCE

One way to understand the context and environments where these companies work is to use TCE analysis (Williamson, 1979, 1991, 1996) where the relationships between suppliers and manufacturers are central. TCE ultimately simplifies the relationship to a contractual problem where the focus is on transaction cost or '*the cost of running the economic system*' (Arrow, 1969, p. 48). Here, the basic assumptions are that companies are embedded in uncertain operational environments (or markets) and operate with bounded rationality,[1] actors act opportunistically, and everything is scaled down to a contractual problem. The theory has three dimensions for its explanations: asset specificity,[2] uncertainty, and transaction frequency. In the hostage model of Williamson, there are alternatives of how this is played out (1985, pp. 170–175). The demand model is stochastic and the buyer can take or refuse delivery. The main point is that the buyer is the dominant and active player who controls how asset specificity is owned and invested and has the best information and therefore less uncertainty, while the supplier becomes a passive instrument in the transaction.

To secure the interest and cooperation of the supplier, and to prevent bounded rationality and opportunism merging, contrived cancellation, uncertain valuation, and incomplete contracting must be analyzed. Contrived cancellation reveals many nuances of opportunism. One part can withhold information that is vital for the contract and relation, but at the same time fulfill its obligations or a perfunctory fulfillment when a close cooperation would be needed (Clarkson, Miller, & Muris, 1978; Williamson, 1985). Williamson suggests that offering a hostage will sort things out in many cases: '*a king who is known to cherish two daughters equally and is asked, for screening purposes, to post a hostage is better advised to offer the ugly one*' (1985, p. 177). In the case company this is a dilemma, how much information should you give to the OEM? Too much information can enable the OEM to set up production in low-cost countries with the technology of C6.

Uncertain valuation looks at the specific investment k, which is assumed to be well specified. The assumption is a great simplification of reality, especially when the investment is human knowledge, which is often tacit knowledge or tacit knowing (Ichijo & Nonaka, 2007; Nonaka, 1994; Polanyi, 1958, 1966; Von Krogh, Ichijo, & Nonaka, 2000). The value of tacit knowing is most often based on historical use of the knowledge and the ability to make good use of insight (Polanyi, 1958, 1966). Even in the process of setting value on physical assets, differences may occur, for example, due to varying legislation, the tax value differs from the value in the financial statement, and so on. There are many aspects of hostage offering and taking that complicate the picture. A producer can use the hostage to integrate into the buyer's market, producers can feign a delivery competence, and so on. The risk involved in hostage taking and offering will adjust the terms in the contract (Williamson, 1985, 1996). C6 often received production tools as a hostage but had to commit to cutting prices throughout production, which can be seen in its offer of hostages toward the OEM.

An incomplete contract is the last factor to be analyzed in terms of the interest and cooperation of the supplier. Contracts are most often incomplete due to unforeseen contingencies, or maladapted due to contractual adjustments when unforeseen contingencies occur that are mistaken or wrong. This is often the case when the parties acquire deeper knowledge of production and demand during the execution of a contract (Nelson & Winter, 1982; Williamson, 1985). Incomplete contracts will leave space for producer haggling. Williamson's answer to this problem of haggling and incomplete contracting is specialized governance structures which promote '*harmonious adaptations and preser[ve] the continuity of exchange relations*' (1985, p. 178). The two suggested solutions are arbitration and reciprocal exposure of the specialized assets. In the case company, the OEM offers the quality system and project management system to secure cooperation, deals with unforeseen events, acquires deeper knowledge about production and contract execution, and—last but not least—maintains relationship governance.

Some alternative safeguards are also mentioned by Williamson (1985, p. 179):

- Full compensation upon order cancellation, in which event buyers are exposed to expropriation hazards
- Buyers invest in specific assets but refuse compensation, which creates a more favorable demand scenario but still offers suppliers the (reduced) risk of uncompensated losses
- As a compromise, suppliers create credible commitments and make partial but incomplete hostage payments upon order cancellation
- The contractual relation is expanded by developing suitable reciprocity arrangements

These options are both interesting and important in a contractual context, but less so when knowledge creation and learning in the relationship are in focus.

TCE is a static pie-sharing theory with limited insight into consequences and means for the working environment. However, it can describe how the case companies relate to their customers, on which they are very dependent. Most often, the customer owns the production tools where the producer is based. It represents a kind of hostage, that is, '*if you do not do as I tell you to do, I will take back all my tools and give it to somebody else.*' This is a direct hostage, but there are also indirect ones that follow the power balance of the direct. For example, '*you shall use my quality system, schemas, and project management system, and answer me on every enquiry I make.*' For an independent company, it becomes a very dependent position. In addition, it affects much more than the actual transaction. Looking at this from a cultural perspective will give a different, more dynamic understanding of this transactional system working in a truly global setting. It starts with the framework of splitting.

The Notion of Splitting

The notion of 'splitting' originates in psychology and deals with how individuals bring the world together in a cohesive and—for them—realistic way by looking at positive and negative qualities of the self and others. It was developed by Fairbairn (Scharff & Scharff, 2005) through his work on object relations theory. It ultimately deals with instabilities in relationships. The individual can judge another person as something good, of personified virtue, or something bad which depends on the person's ability to gratify individual needs or frustrations at any given time. Splitting is recognized as a common defense mechanism within people who have personality disorders (Zanarini, Weingeroff, & Frankenburg, 2009). However, Klein expanded the idea of splitting to objects (Segal, 1992). People can have a good or bad relationship to an object. The value of the relationship to a specific object refers to the experience associated with it. A good experience means that an object is good, a bad experience means that an object is bad. As its usage embraces both people and objects, splitting can be used as a structured background to understand the value chain in an organizational culture and structure perspective. The culture deals mainly with people and their fantasies or realities, while structure focuses on objects. Splitting as dividing good and bad associations of people and objects fits well into the differentiated perspective of culture.

Using splitting allows us to deal with an analytical problem. Previously, I explained how differences in espoused theory and theory-in-use eventually lead to defensive actions. Other ways of explaining could be by claiming that people lie and resist new ideas. However, splitting allows us to say that people are not stupid or mean. They are not clear who is responsible for what, although when things are not going well it is tempting to blame it on somebody else, which is not unusual but still a problem that needs to be solved by managing it better.

Differentiated Perspective of Culture

This dependency by operating in a global industry and how it affects culture will be illustrated by analyzing different short stories. The matrix form of Martin will serve as a guide throughout.

> The manifestations of cultures in organizations include formal and informal practices, cultural forms (such as rituals, stories, jargon, humor, and physical arrangements), and content themes. Interpretations of these cultural manifestations vary. The pattern or configuration of interpretations (underlying a matrix of cultural manifestations) constitutes culture. (1992, pp. 37–38)

This is a definition of culture and an argument for using a matrix analysis as a guide through stories about culture. The matrix uses content themes, practices, and forms as the basic categories. It is a simple analysis that can shed light on important sides of organizational culture. However, we intend to simplify it even further and then disagree with Martin by broadening and amplifying her differentiated perspective by adding more dimensions. In this effort, merely showing a matrix analysis will not make much sense. Instead, we will start with listing the different stories that will follow with a brief comment:

- Student visit—illustrate the CEO's position as both boss and servant in an environment with high pressure
- Conventional industry—illustrate 'us and them' thinking
- Change orders and language—show contradictory demands, high development pressure, and the providence of a special language
- The Easter Action—a war/hero story focusing on the hero as a great problem-solver
- The Christmas Action—also a war story turning into a hero story. However, here the result is a new simulation program which is believed to be a major competitive advantage. Both war stories conclude in a section dealing with spillover effects from the proverb
- Engineers as craftsman—analyze the behavior of the engineers
- Task teams and subcultural boundaries—show how different subcultures having different ways of creating knowledge
- Types of developers—posits that even inside a subculture there are contradictions and different ways of creating knowledge
- Voice of the customer—deals with the importance of the customer demands and different ways of working with the customer as motivating factors for response times and relationships

Specifically, after task teams and subcultural boundaries, we offer an analysis based on Geertz's (1973) writing of religion definition for emphasizing internal business contradictions. It is used to highlight multiple Geertzian cultures that work under the structure of the larger, shared environment. However, each of these diverse and deviant cultures have their own dynamics that involve sense-making. Managing this diversity and sense-making puts a great constraint on management. In this environment with diverse and deviant cultures, joint decision-making and voting will not solve problems. This cultural analysis points toward the need for special management—the facilitative management. These topics are discussed in detail in the chapters of internal contradictions and facilitative management.

Student's Visit

As teachers of the university, the research team arranged a visit to C6 for some undergraduate students. During the CEO's presentation of the company, his phone rang. He picked it up, looked at it, and then turned it off. When talking to the audience, he commented that it was a Korean car manufacturer calling on a pressing issue. When asked to students afterwards, nobody reflected on the incident as something special. However, his employees and the research team were baffled. This behavior was, for us, extraordinary. While talking to the employees who were present, they all commented that not answering a customer's call is almost a sin. However, there is more to this story than a CEO doing something wrong in the eyes of the employees. As already mentioned, C6 deeply depends on its customers. It is an asymmetric relationship and this is obvious when looking at the behavior of the CEO and the reaction from the insiders to it.

His behavior must be understood considering the asymmetrical relationship. The OEM, in this case a Korean car manufacturer, owns the production tools and demands that its quality system and project management systems are used. A quality system in automotive industry is huge; for instance, the manual for filling in the FMEA form is 290 pages with very detailed descriptions. This form is just one of many, and each OEM has their own way concerning quality reporting. It is a massive undertaking to understand, learn, and follow up one such system. The authority and action space of the CEO toward the customer is therefore limited. Ultimately, he and his company will do what the customer demands. Internally, the CEO's authority and action space are much greater, but it is still connected to the asymmetrical relationship with the customer. To become a supplier in the automotive industry, it is common to agree to yearly decreasing prices, from 5 to 7 percent. Thus, in order to make profit the supplier must continually improve production while meeting yearly decreasing prices. It puts the CEO and his organization under great pressure. When the Korean car manufacturer called, the CEO responded to this by switching his phone off. In the sense of splitting, he categorized the Korean car manufacturer as bad because they kept nagging him about one particular incident. In light of the splitting, the CEO defended his actions. However, his employees saw this action as something wrong. Later, they responded in interviews that they could never do something like that although getting them to explain their reasoning was difficult; it was just something you do not do. Nevertheless, one employee responded by saying that they could lose their jobs. In talking with others, this seemed to be the argument, which again returns to the asymmetrical relationship. It illustrates the difficult leading role of the CEO as boss and servant. He has the legitimacy to lead but little scope for action, while on an individual level experienced splitting.

CONVENTIONAL INDUSTRY

In the Raufoss cluster, many stories are told which serve different purposes, but here we concentrate on two main categories: hero and war stories. Hero stories have two main purposes: telling newcomers how things are done and idealizing certain behaviors. War stories are most often used to create an internal identity against others/external actors. You need to know these stories in order to become a fully-fledged member of the group.

A common war story is the variant where the company compares themselves with 'conventional industry.' The fascinating part of such stories is that the company most often knows little about the 'conventional industry,' and in many ways is not conventional itself. A much-used phrase at Raufoss is that they compete in the most competitive global market successfully, namely, the automotive industry. It is true that the automotive industry is both global and competitive; however, the most competitive is questionable. We have never seen any proof to support such a claim, but it is used extensively to promote governmental interest for making better competitive conditions for the manufacturing industry. Another tactic is to recount how clever the companies are for 'surviving against all odds,' located in one of the most expensive countries in the world and still manage to survive due to continuous flows of technological innovations. One European OEM got a new development leader. He called in all the suppliers and told them that now they had to cut prices. The time of high profits was over. With a simple technological innovation, fitting the robot arm with the dual grips, C3 managed to overcome this price-cutting and double production. Similar stories have occurred over the history of car-making. However, many of these war stories turn into hero stories. The hero in this story managed with minimum investments to overcome the changed demand from the customer. It was a creative answer to the constant threatening environment with changing demands.

CHANGE ORDERS

Major changes in a product-development project that the customer initiated will normally come as change orders. A recent study at C3 (Lodgaard, Larsson, & Ringen, 2013) investigated change orders in 16 different development projects. They found that it varied from one to 157 change orders from the customers. However, the average was 43, and keeping in mind that a normal project duration is two years, this is a lot of work. Another study showed that 77 percent of all 'change orders' are internal (Shankar, Morkos, & Summers, 2012), making up for even more work and rework. It therefore seems like it is a dynamic environment with constant pressures and contradictory demands.

Turning the focus back to C6, a similar war story that ends up as a hero story is set at the beginning of the company's history. At that time, C6 had just finished developing its first product to an American car manufacturer, but realized that it was difficult to gain profit due to heavy investments and a lengthy development period. When it transpired that the car platform[3] did not reach the volumes that the American car manufacturer's figures said, the sale was half of the volume budget. C6 had invested in a factory that could cope with the high original estimates of an American car manufacturer, and now only produced at half its capacity. Still, the American car manufacturer demanded steadily decreasing prices. A natural answer to this existential threat and pressure is to look for more customers, and it did with a creative product solution: cutting the standard aluminum profile, pressing the ends, drilling holes, welding on a tap, and ending up with a low-price product (a suspension arm). A Korean car manufacturer was the first customer for this low-price product. C6 managed to produce a suspension part in a high-cost country, export it to a low-cost one (South Korea) to be placed in a low-price car (a Korean car manufacturer). Again, we see a story about a demanding customer triggering a possible crisis that people in the organization respond to with new and innovative technological solutions. For C6 this was the starting point of obtaining more customers. In Survey #1, we asked about how many projects each developer worked in (Fig. 4.1).

The majority of people working at C6 were involved in two to four projects simultaneously, but there were many, about 27 percent, who had five to ten. Adding to this is the fact that there is seldom more than one ongoing project with one individual customer. Therefore, participating in four projects means reporting in and 'talking' four different 'languages.' There are at least four different project management ways. Having a delay

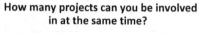

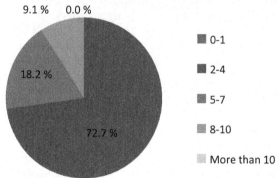

Fig. 4.1   Project involvement

in one project will easily interfere with another lead by a different leader. However, C6 cannot tell a Swedish car manufacturer there is a delay because some other competitor of them needs something now. Therefore, explaining such delays are difficult, and many times members feel it is an unpleasant task. In short, people at the development department were exposed to contradictory demands, constant threats of failing, and constant pressures. These factors characterize working life.

Being involved in different projects with different 'languages' demands a lot of everyone. To give an example, an American car manufacturer issued an excel file with over 400 pages of explanations with the abbreviations and acronyms that are most common. Even if you are familiar with the language used, the forms and reports still do not tell the entire story as they only draw conclusions in the form of clues, and do not even use full sentences. When we presented this to the people at the R&D department at C6, they agreed, though it came as somewhat of a surprise as they had never previously thought of it this way before. Change orders are putting the development project in a constant backwards loop. One incident in the Swedish car manufacturer project occurred relatively late in the project. The technological design was finished and plans for industrialization were underway. The Swedish car manufacturer called one morning for a phone conference[4] on a bad telephone line. It wanted to move a mounting bracket some centimeters further back which meant a redesign with new drawings, and the FMEA process and all the testing had to be redone.

A huge amount of work was wasted for merely moving a mounting bracket. Adding this to the other changes during the duration of a project, it can be very a frustrating place to work, that is: '*What you have done today you need to rework tomorrow, just because the customer says so.*' In addition, with lots of changes the possibility to fail increases. Just one recall of a faulty part in a car model could mean economic ruin for C6. This fact is something that the organization is aware of and intensifies the pressure felt. The people at C3 who develop crash boxes[5] have morbid humor about this: '*If a crash box fails then there is nobody left to complain.*' Besides being morbid, it is a way of saying that they are glad not to have this threat of possible recalls hanging over their heads.

THE EASTER ACTION

The following story was one that a newcomer to Raufoss would hear. However, s/he would only hear bits and pieces, and not the entire story. To get the entire story, an interview with the actual 'hero' was arranged. This interview was scheduled for two hours but took a full day, with very detailed technological descriptions left out here because of space constraints.

The story is known as the Easter action as most of it played out during the Easter vacation. After the development of the lower front control arm,[6] complaints came from the customer of bushings that loosened. Quite a bit of effort went into solving this problem. At first, only a few out of the thousands produced loosened, so it was difficult to pinpoint the problem. However, some improvements were made, and hope was that these actions would solve the problem. At some point after the improvements, the problem reoccurred at the Italian car manufacturer's assembly line. Faulty parts were then sent to C6, but no production faults were found after rigorous testing and analyses. The company decided to go to the Italian car manufacturer assembly line and talk to the people in charge to obtain more information. A senior developer (the hero in this story) led the C6 delegation. After some lengthy discussions in a meeting room that led nowhere, our developer asked if he could see the assembly line, especially where the control arm was attached to the frame and the rest of the suspension. Walking the line, he noticed that someone clever on the line had installed a time-saving device for mounting the control arm to the rest of the suspension. The arm has an extension pin at the ball joint that fits into a socket with a spring mechanism to hold it in place. A wooden club is usually used to manually hammer the pin into the socket, but the Italian car manufacturer had realized that the bushings in the arm could be used as a spring; by bending the arm down and releasing, it would spring up into the socket with just the right amount of force. It was clever, and saved lots of manual labor and time on the line. Looking closer at this innovative solution, the senior developer measured the angle that the control arm was bending down at before it released into the socket above. The angle was at the maximum of 27 degrees. Remembering that the customer had specified some tolerance in the working of the control arm, the senior developer went back to his notes and found that the control arm was developed to have a maximum bending angle of 17 degrees. After establishing this fact, the assembly line had to be rebuilt, and the claims from the customer were withdrawn.

This story of the Easter action is told with many variations within the company and the cluster at Raufoss. Nevertheless, for these purposes, it served as an insight into why the hero status was built and how the engineers and developers like to see themselves. It is communicated to newcomers as an ideal. Besides achieving hero status, this story indicates the desire to be great problem-solvers in the company, but more importantly for the customer. Identity of the experts is linked to meaningful contribution for the customer. The ability to solve problems, even during holidays, is highly regarded. Remembering a little specification detail in an ocean of customer requirements is part of the problem-solver's ability. Interestingly, the fact that the hero had saved the company from a very costly recall of parts that could have easily led to bankruptcy is only tacitly understood. This is never told as part of the story, and every time we have encountered the story, it has stopped before coming to this fact. It is the engineering problem-solving achievement that is talked about and celebrated, and how this helped the customer is highlighted. Therefore, it is natural to conclude that the engineering problem-solving ability is strongly part of the identity of these experts. Another important part of the story is the characteristic of how quickly the problem was solved. This runs counter to the general understanding of the quality system theory, and in some sense, the Lean tradition also focus on problem-solving tools[7] that need to be applied to find its root cause. The identity that follows the story is of a lonely engineer who solves complex problems by having the entire complex details in his/her head.

The Christmas Action

Another well-known story in the development community at Raufoss goes under the name of the Christmas action. The company behind this story was C3. The project was the development of the bumper and crash boxes for the German sports car sports car, which was not itself an important project, but the new platform for the volume family cars market that were due to be announced in just a short time. Succeeding with the sports car project was believed to be the key to landing the bigger order of the family cars, which are produced in much greater numbers than the sports car. Due to its low volume, a simpler solution for the sport's car was agreed upon that should have been a straightforward development project with low production cost. A new test—the pole test—was introduced early in the project, but as the development team did not believe it to be an important issue, it was (re)scheduled for a later stage in the development process. In short, the test was a simulation of a car crashing into an obstacle, in this case a pole, at a certain speed and the bumper should absorb the impact by not bending too much. If the bumper intrusion was too great, it would damage the costlier components in the car. Running the test just before Christmas, a catastrophe struck. The car tore off the welds and a catastrophic failure was the result. Huge resources were put into investigating and correcting the design before the next official attempt to clear the pole test. Two engineers, including one with a PhD degree, were frenetically testing different design solutions at the internal test center during the Christmas break. To cut a long story short, they finally went for a much more expensive solution and succeeded. As many had anticipated, the bigger order of the family car platform was granted to C3, in part because of succeeding in the new pole test.

Again, there are many versions of the Christmas action story, but this short one is based on an interview with the test engineer involved (who holds a PhD) and his boss at the time. Still, there is the belief that a great engineer must be a great problem-solver, never take time off, and solve the issue or crisis quickly and efficiently, thereby helping to secure the next much bigger order. However, the bad decision that led to the crisis and postponed the test to the end of the development process is left out when the story is retold. Nonetheless, the people interviewed were very honest and sincere about this. What sets this story apart from the other one is the result: a very sophisticated computer simulation program for tearing off welds in a crash test. The development department at C3 is very proud of this, which they believe is a significant competitive advantage as well as shows the ability to learn from failure, needed to be successful.

CONCLUSION OF ACTION STORIES

There are of course many more action stories, as well as stories rooted in different parts of the company such as production. The two told here give an idea of storytelling in a product-development department, giving rise to a proverb: '*Crises create heroes.*' The meaning is that a crisis can be solved, and they are quite capable of solving crises at Raufoss.[8] A hero is a great problem-solver. Analyzing this proverb more deeply, Elster points out the importance of the net effect of the proverb, rather than looking for the cause of it (2007, p. 40). The net effect of the stories can be solutions to compete in a global marketplace. This net effect is something that people in the small community of the companies are proud of. Even so, it is interesting to look at how the stories have affected the foundation for knowledge creation and learning. Moreover, how we use the tools at hand to develop new knowledge and learn is seemingly the foundation for these companies' competitive advantage. Elster also argues for the importance of looking at the proverb's spillover effect (2007, pp. 42–44). Here, at least two can be imagined:

1. It does not matter whether we follow the company's rules or quality systems as we can fix the crisis anyway. In addition, if a crisis occurs, we can become heroes.
2. Analytic tools to find the root cause of a problem are not very well regarded because they can reveal that it was the hero who caused the crisis to occur in the first place.

The cultural effect of the storytelling is that it is desirable to become a hero, and as a hero you do not need to follow strict problem-solving tools or what the quality system requires. Quality systems are implemented so that the less experienced—non-hero—knows what to do. In practice, the speed of problem-solving is highly regarded. A hero needs to solve problems fast and without tools. When s/he sees the problem, s/he can explain rather quickly why it has occurred and how to fix it. Such speedy problem-solving was mentioned several times when interviewing product developers. This is fascinating because it suggests to us that a notion of craft knowledge inspires these engineers, and that they see the quality rules as necessary for apprentices and journeymen. In other words, engineers are masters and other employees are apprentices. Engineers like to describe themselves as scientific thinkers; however, they commonly behave in the way of a master craftsman. Seeing the procedures of the quality systems as something that stifles their creative activity can serve as a clue. Another clue is their dismissal of the other workers as novices and journeymen who do not have the brainpower and experience to question their authority. Thus, inside this apparent scientific environment of high pressure and Total Quality Management (TQM), you can see all the old ideologies that structure bad relations among different categories of workers.

ENGINEERS AS CRAFTSMEN

Richard Sennett (2008) discusses the idea of craftsmanship or the skill of resolving issues. This notion has to do with the cultural issue of technique, in which a central point is the desire to do a job well for its own sake. But, there are many things that stand in the way of doing the job well, for example, a lack of good tools, excessive bureaucratization, a lack of training, inadequate education, and so on. Putting the notion of craftsman in perspective, Sennett (2008) comes up with three dimensions: skill, commitment, and judgment.

When someone is good at something, s/he conducts a dialogue between concrete practices and thinking; a good example of this would be the behavior of a carpenter where s/he can 'feel' the nails go in correctly or not, or a blacksmith who can 'hear' if the steel is at the right temperature when hammering. In business practices such as product development and marketing, more abstract skills involve a duality in work. Technical understanding is only possible when skills are developed through the power of imagination and language is the very tool for imagining as it enables one person to tell another what works best: '*The use of imperfect or incomplete tools draws on the imagination in developing the skills to repair and to improvise*' (Sennett, 2008). These two faculties—practice and imagination—are intuitively grasped, but developing such skills is arduous. The role of imagination is a particularly interesting issue. It is central to the problem-solver's celebrated ability.

Commitment deals with motivation and talent. A talented person will not do well if s/he is not motivated, but a motivated person can do well without being a great talent. The danger is when motivation transforms into obsession whereby '*[t]he obsession with getting things perfectly right may deform the work itself*' (Sennett, 2008). Developing the ability to manage obsession eases the process of developing expertise. To become a hero, talent is believed to be involved as the hero appears to be able to remember huge amounts of detail, for example, nailing the root cause in its head, and so on. In addition, customer satisfaction drives the hero's problem-solving and motivates him or her.

Judgment deals with the ethical side of craftsmanship[9]: 'The good craftsman ... uses solutions to uncover new territory; problem-solving and problem finding are intimately related in his or her mind' (Sennett, 2008). A craftsman can ask both why and how, while concurrently standing back and evaluating the work ethics. The last point is more of an individual choice. Judgment is closely connected to solving customers' problems, but not by using their prescribed systems. Documenting the problem in prescribed systems is believed to be too time-consuming and does not address the problem correctly, etc. The developers tend to ask both why and how in their own way, forgetting that shortcuts can lead to additional employer costs. Finally, ethics deals with self-assertion in the eyes of the customer and other developers at Raufoss.

These three dimensions show how the craft mentality resists the ideology behind the quality and management systems. In these systems, the prescribed way of doing things should secure prefect products first time around. In addition, the systems are seen as helping novices rather than the full-blown hero such as the 'scientific engineer' or master craftsman who is not interested in the science that involves filling out quality forms.

CONCLUSION INCONSISTENCIES

Some other revelations occur when looking at these stories through the lens of Martin's (1992) differentiated culture dimension. Martin's notions of inconsistencies are divided into action, symbolic, and ideological (1992, pp. 85–88). Action inconsistency is similar to Argyris and Schön's (1996) arguments about differences between espoused theory and theory-in-action, where the actual practice does not follow espoused content theme. In storytelling, actions are promoted that differ from what should be done according to quality and management systems. However, there is more to it than just rule-breaking. It reveals an 'underbelly' of conflict. These stories center on well-known, highly respected engineers who solve problems by not using the prescribed problem-solving tools for project management. Still, they solve problems for customer satisfaction. The conflict then lies in the unwillingness to use the prescribed tools. One argument that the research team frequently encountered was that such tools were perceived to inhibit creativity. The evidence for this relates back to the stories previously described. Nevertheless, it also points to a conflict of cross-functional teams and teamwork for problem-solving. Managerial rhetoric does not fit these stories at all, in line with the arguments of Jermier (1991) and Kunda (2006). Kunda clearly states an alternative to the task management control (Fuller, 2002) and the Lean concept of standardization (Womack & Jones, 1996). These stories are about solitary and individual efforts that make hero status in the environment. As for ideological inconsistency, it can be argued that action and symbolically inconsistent behavior, which is celebrated as successful problem-solving to secure future contracts, threatens employees' job security. The Christmas action failed to understand the importance of the pole test and postponed it. This decision was based on few facts, thereby not following the rules and routines. The later celebrated efforts of frantic testing could have been avoided if the decision was initially based on facts. In addition, the outcome could not have ended so successfully, setting the next huge contract in danger.

Listening to these stories from the managers, along with the speech of sticking to routines and rules set in the quality and management systems, represent ideological inconsistency as behaviors are highlighted that contradict the main points of the systems' message. In addition, this accountability-based quality control, celebrated by the Lean and TQM movements, does not produce quality. It pretends to describe actions that are much more complicated and may well provoke behavior against quality goals through 'soldiering' or active resistance, such as in the organizational learning model O-I. However, this is not the answer. Quality starts with the actual work done. Filling out forms for documentation is not quality; it is merely documentation. Quality works best when the documents can be used as tools in the ongoing work.

TASK TEAMS AND SUBCULTURAL BOUNDARIES

In the section of organizational learning, FMEA was used as an example. Here, it was briefly mentioned in the task teams, that is, groups put together to solve pressing problems, which have members from different organizational functions but appear to be led by people from the development department. Survey #1 leads us to believe that the product-development department has some strong personalities that dominate discussions and decisions. Having these people in task teams means two subcultures colliding. Specifically, people from production were hands-on and—when interviewing—eager to demonstrate what they are doing by pointing at the machines, showing programs, and so on. Yet, common practice is to document every stop and discuss every improvement at length before its implementation. Improvement suggestions take time to implement and discuss because several shifts need to be agreed upon. In the restrooms, vital information about production is displayed using charts, diagrams, photos, and tables. These symbols show the work activity and often focus the professional conversation by an established language. Charts, diagrams, and so on are used in the handover meetings between shifts and to set the formal agenda, but the meetings are far more informal. However, a newcomer or an outsider needs to understand these objects in order to be listened to or have a say as they represent the formal knowledge and espoused actions of the company, just as the writing in any holy book is a guideline for individuals' actions. However, the actions in practice are often different.

The attitude toward the computer program, which serves as the input base for the charts and such like, illustrates the differences in practice well. Documentation is created in the program with standardized texts to choose from, and comments added if required. However, there was resentment toward the documentation. Specifically, when the research team asked about its usage the operators went silent, rolling their eyes and commenting: '*When there are several stops in rapid succession, what is then important—getting the line up and running or documenting it in the system?*' This was followed by '*in the standardized text we have to choose from, often there are no real good alternatives, and we do not have the time to write whole stories in the commentary field either.*'

On the other hand, people from the development department have engineering degrees (some even PhDs) and they were very good at articulating themselves. They also have lots of charts, diagrams, and so on that seemingly show how they work, but are in reality function more as symbols of espoused actions or guidelines and their subculture is more diverse. One example regards people conducting theoretical stress analysis (FEM—Finite Element Method) who can be divided into two different groups,[10] entirely identifying themselves with neither the physical testing section nor the quality one. Many of these differences go along with knowledge and evidence boundaries. For example, dynamic stresses analysis is a theoretical model of a structure, while the testers can claim its actual proof as they physically test the model. The theoretical FEM analysts do calculations in an abstract environment and the testers are proud of being practical, sometimes enjoying having the final answer over theoretical FEM analysts. The quality control group, however, feels 'left in the shadows.' The company had steadily reduced the number of people in this group, arguing that they should only guide the developers. The rationale behind this is that quality starts at the source, which is a classical argument that can be found in different ways within the literature (Freyssenet, Mair,

Shimizu, & Volpato, 1998; Liker, 2004; Mair, 1998; Shimizu, 1998). One classical argument following this rationale is the discussion between Ohno, the father of Toyota Production System (TPS), and Nemoto, the father of Total Quality Control at Toyota. Ohno's argued that quality starts by making the operator responsible for his or her work by demanding perfection. On the other hand, Nemoto argued that this is important, but the company needs defined goals to lead the organization, Hoshin Kanri as they called it, or TQM.[11] Now TPS and TQM are two legs in the quality work at Toyota and equally important (Shimokawa & Fujimoto, 2010). In C6, the quality group felt that they had been reduced to a consultancy role of lower importance than the other groups in the development department. This potentially paved the way for a disaster by giving an impression of quality management when there is none which ultimately contributes the possibility of bad managerial decision-making as data bore no resemblance to reality. Developers, as such, are skeptical toward operators' critique of design issues that do not comply with mass production. The same can be said for the operators who did not like having academics tell them what to do, although reluctantly admitted that it sometimes helped.

CONCLUSION

This chapter started by providing an understanding of the asymmetrical relationship between supplier and OEM. To some degree, this explains the special relationship and the usage of quality and project management systems. Following this, it turned to splitting for dealing with an analytical problem which explains seemingly irrational behavior without saying that people are at fault. Splitting explained the behavior of the CEO during a student visit to the factory and offers a glimpse into the demanding relationship a supplier has in the automotive industry. The CEO is not just a boss, but also a servant at the same time. More evidence of the difficult relationship between the supplier and OEM are offered in the comparison of 'us' against conventional industry. It also shows the spirit of 'competing against the odds.' Even more evidence is provided in the change order section whereby a pattern of contradictory demands emerges. Combining contradictory demands with huge workloads via participation in many simultaneous projects with different quality and project management systems paints the picture of a difficult and stressful work place for all developers, not only the CEO. Two war stories that turned into stories about heroes illustrate the ideal engineer through the eyes of developers as great problem-solvers that save the company in times of crises. The proverb '*crisis create heroes*' therefore has two spillover effects: (a) heroes do not have to follow the rules or use the quality systems because of their 'superior' knowledge position; and (b) analytical tools are not well regarded because they can reveal who initially caused the crisis. It also provides a clue for understanding the engineers as craftsmen rather than scientific thinkers. These craftsmen are analyzed in three dimensions: skill, commitment, and judgment. Furthermore, this craft mentality resists the ideology behind the quality and management systems, and the 'scientific engineer' or master craftsman shows little interest in documentation.

Further, the hero stories demonstrate the three dimensions of inconsistency: action, symbolic, and ideological. Actions are twofold regarding what is said to have been done and what has actually been done. This inconsistency reveals an 'underbelly' of conflict illustrated by an unwillingness to use the prescribed tools by claiming they inhibit creativity. However, the argument about the creativity points toward a conflict of cross-functional teams and teamwork for problem-solving. Such team rhetoric does not fit with the status of hero-making as a contextual symbol. Furthermore, the ideological inconsistencies are the result of action and symbolically inconsistent behavior, setting future contracts in danger and threatening employees' job security. These dimensions are discussed in the stories of task teams and subcultural boundaries. However, the conclusion is that accountability-based quality control does not produce quality. Until now, the chapter agrees with the differentiated culture dimension.

NOTES

1. Rationality is bounded in a limited and intentional way (Coase, 1984; Simon, 1972, 1982) or as Williamson argued: '...an economizing orientation is elicited by the intended rationality ..., while the study of institutions is encouraged by conceding that cognitive competence is limited' (1985, p. 45).
2. Asset specificity is the result of supporting a particular transaction and limited value outside the specific transactions parties.
3. Cars are built on platforms, everything the consumers do not see can be thought of as a platform. For example, Epsilon 1 was the platform for Opel Vectra, Saab 93, and Fiat Chroma.
4. Because this was in the middle of the financial crisis, traveling expenses were cut and phone conferences were used instead.

5. Crash boxes absorb lots of the energy in a collision and direct the forces away from the passengers.
6. A part of the wheel suspension.
7. Example: 5 times why, fishbone diagram, and so on.
8. Can also be looked at as firefighting in projects.
9. The example Sennett (2008) gives pertains to Oppenheimer, the father of the nuclear, who was a brilliant physicist and researcher, but the result of his work was not good for mankind.
10. This is explained in detail later in this chapter.
11. TQM here includes Total Quality Control (TQC) that sees the quality efforts through leaders' eyes.

REFERENCES

Argyris, C., & Schön, D. (1996). *Organizational learning II: Theory, method, and practice*. Reading: Addison-Wesley Publishing Company.

Arrow, K. (1969). *The organization of economic activity: Issues pertinent to the choice of market versus nonmarket allocation*. Paper presented at the analysis and evaluation of public expenditure, PPB System, Washington.

Clarkson, K. W., Miller, R. L., & Muris, T. J. (1978). Liquidated damages v. penalties. *Wisconsin Law Review, 54,* 351–390.

Coase, R. H. (1984). The new institutional economics. *Journal of Institutional and Theoretical Economics, 140,* 229–231.

Elster, J. (2007). *Explaining social behavior: More nuts and bolts for the social sciences*. Cambridge: Cambridge University Press.

Freyssenet, M., Mair, A., Shimizu, K., & Volpato, G. (1998). *One best way? Trajectories and industrial models of the world's automobile producers*. Oxford: Oxford University Press.

Fuller, S. (2002). *Knowledge management foundations*. Boston, MA: Butterworth-Heinemann.

Geertz, C. (1973). *The interpretation of cultures*. New York: Basic Books.

Ichijo, K., & Nonaka, I. (2007). *Knowledge creation and management*. Oxford: Oxford University Press.

Jermier, J. M. (1991). Critical epistemology and the study of organizational culture: Reflections on street corner society. In P. J. Frost et al. (Eds.), *Reframing organizational culture* (pp. 223–233). Newbury Park, CA: Sage.

Kunda, G. (2006). *Engineering culture: Control and commitment in a high-tech corporation*. Philadelphia, PA: Temple University Press.

Liker, J. (2004). *The Toyota way: 14 management principles from the world's greatest manufacturer*. New York: McGraw-Hill.

Lodgaard, E., Larsson, C. E., & Ringen, G. (2013). *Viewing the engineering change process from a Lean product development and a business perspective*. Not yet published.

Mair, A. (1998). The globalization of Honda's product-led flexible mass production system. In M. Freyssenet, A. Mair, K. Shimizu, & G. Volpato (Eds.), *One best way?* (pp. 110–138). Oxford: Oxford University Press.

Martin, J. (1992). *Cultures in organizations: Three perspectives.* New York: Oxford University Press.

Nelson, R. R., & Winter, S. G. (1982). *An evolutionary theory of economic change.* Cambridge, MA: Harvard University Press.

Nonaka, I. (1994). A dynamic theory of organizational knowledge creation. *Organization Science, 5*(1), 14–37.

Polanyi, M. (1958). *Personal knowledge.* Chicago, IL: The University of Chicago Press.

Polanyi, M. (1966). *The Tacit dimension.* London: Routledge & Kegan Paul.

Scharff, J. S., & Scharff, D. E. (2005). *The legacy of Fairbairn and Sutherland: Psychotherapeutic applications.* London: Routledge.

Segal, J. (1992). *Melanie Klein.* London: Sage.

Sennett, R. (2008). *The craftsman.* New Haven, CT: Yale University Press.

Shankar, P., Morkos, B., & Summers, J. D. (2012). Reasons for change propagation: A case study in an automotive OEM. *Research in Engineering, 23,* 291–303.

Shimizu, K. (1998). A new Toyotaism. In M. Freyssenet, A. Mair, K. Shimizu, & G. Volpato (Eds.), *One best way?* (pp. 63–90). Oxford: Oxford University Press.

Shimokawa, K., & Fujimoto, T. (2010). *The birth of Lean.* Cambridge, MA: Lean Enterprise Institute.

Simon, H. (1972). Theories of bounded rationality. In C. B. McGuire & R. Radner (Eds.), *Decision and organization.* Amsterdam: North-Holland Publishing Company.

Simon, H. (1982). *Models of bounded rationality* (Vols. 1–2). Cambridge, MA: MIT Press.

Von Krogh, G., Ichijo, K., & Nonaka, I. (2000). *Enabling knowledge creation. How to unlock the mystery of tacit knowledge and release the power of innovation.* Oxford: Oxford University Press.

Williamson, O. (1979). Transaction-cost economics: The governance of contractual relations. *Journal of Law & Economics, 22*(2), 233–261.

Williamson, O. (1985). *The economic institutions of capitalism.* New York: The Free Press.

Williamson, O. (1991). Comparative economic organization: The analysis of discrete structural alternatives. *Administrative Science Quarterly, 36*(2), 269–296.

Williamson, O. (1996). *The mechanisms of governance.* New York: Oxford University Press.

Womack, J. P., & Jones, D. T. (1996). *Lean thinking: Banish waste and create wealth in your corporation.* New York: Free Press.

Zanarini, M. C., Weingeroff, J. L., & Frankenburg, F. R. (2009). Defense mechanisms associated with borderline personality disorder. *Journal of Personality Disorder, 23*(2), 113–121.

CHAPTER 5

Culture: Internal Business Contradictions

Abstract This chapter broadens and deepens insight from the previous chapter by bringing in another theoretical perspective: the Geertzian perspective of culture. It describes how the import of broader global managerial trends affect knowledge-creation processes and the differentiated cultures they are embedded in.

INTRODUCTION

Discussing the differences between sub-cultures and looking at the homogeneity of a sub-culture are illustrated by different types of engineers working with finite element methods in development. This section adds another dimension to Martin's (1992) notion of sub-cultures. The previous chapter dealt with Martin's differentiated perspective in a simplified way. Now this perspective is deviated from in favor of Geertzian Culture in an effort to amplify and broaden Martin's perspective that is suited to multi-causal and multi-dimensional analyses of nested systems. As the voice of the customer is essential for understanding development in the automotive industry, this chapter asks: Who is in direct contact with the customer? How does collaboration with the customer work? And, how does the customer motivate and correct the developers' work? Thereafter, it turns its attention to the sense-making of development processes and systems by looking at how developers construct shared meaning for shared experiences by focusing on the notion of 'dugnad,'[1] further developed in Chap. 6.

© The Author(s) 2018   83
H. Holtskog et al., *Learning Factories*, Palgrave Studies in
Democracy, Innovation, and Entrepreneurship for Growth,
https://doi.org/10.1007/978-3-319-41887-2_5

INTERNAL BUSINESS CONTRADICTIONS

The boundaries between sub-cultures can be separated in different ways regarding their focuses. In operations, the most important things are flow, quality variations, and continuous improvement where various programs and efforts keep the machinery going by controlling quality variations and improving operational information daily. On the other hand, the development department focuses on satisfying new customer needs, problem-solving, and calculations. Throughout a project's history, new demands arrive from the customer as the car's development progresses; changes in parts trigger changes in other parts. When the development of individual car parts are sent to the suppliers or sub-suppliers there is an endless chain of changes that need to be considered. These may produce new problems that can only be solved by new calculations of the impact changes will have on dynamic forces of the car part. Therefore, the focal point of each sub-culture is different, and in some cases could be contradictory; for example, rapid changes do not apply with continuous improvement, therefore leading to stigma between the two sub-cultures whereby the developers were seen to be shortsighted with quick-fix solutions, while operators were seen as dragging solutions out over time.

The boundaries are represented by symbols and meaning which somewhat correspond to Geertz's definition of religion: 'a system of symbols which acts to establish powerful, pervasive, and long-lasting moods and motivations in men by formulating conceptions of a general order of existence and clothing these conceptions with such an aura of factuality that the moods and motivations seem uniquely realistic' (1973, p. 90). As we have seen, the charts, diagrams, and so on are symbols in various sub-cultures and the interpretation of them or the meaning behind establish powerful and pervasive moods and motivations in people. These symbols are believed to represent facts, even when they are aware that the input text does not fit the actual problem and sets realistic goals. However, what makes it difficult is that the symbols are not necessarily the same in every department, with different meanings which can be illustrated by the notion of deadlines. Dates or deadlines in operations, even if these dates represent stress and people acknowledge the importance of keeping them, are equally important to all in the sense that everyone gets the possibility to comment on the work-change and agree. Reaching consensus represents the default obligation that summarizes the symbols. On the other hand, developers have dates and deadlines, often far in the future, and a guided way of making it to that overall date. One such important date, which both developers and operations have in common, is the Start-of-Operation (SOP) where the mass production of a new part starts. Developers guided way to this SOP consists of years of small deadlines and filling in numerous forms and so forth where the decided solution is non-negotiable, unless one can prove it wrong. However, the mentality of the operators is one of consensus as they have not been part of every decided upon solution along the line, and therefore want to discuss its important aspects to better understand and reach agreement. Developers, however, believe this slows the whole process down and makes the dates unreachable. Not making the SOP is a disaster for any project, and going back and questioning old decisions is useless in their minds. Developers reach decisions based on discussion between those involved in the process or those with knowledge of the specific topic; everyone else adjusts and follows the decisions. Consensus is not an issue, but making (seemingly) rational choices that move the projects forward to the SOP is the overall objective. Developers think that the questioning and discussion which operators exhibit is pointless and delays the SOP. On the other hand, operators feel that decision-making is too hasty and do not feel confident that deadlines can be met. They believe that discussions and agreements are vital parts of making a successful SOP, and project leaders, being developers, have not taken this into account.

TYPES OF DEVELOPERS

Determining if a sub-culture is uniform or not, relates to Martin's (1992) differentiated perspective calls for consensus within the sub-culture. Our observations—to some degree—support this; however, this book has a different objective that regards how industry creates knowledge. The central argument for the importance of this difference is that the way people create knowledge influences how they reach consensus within the sub-culture. In addition, this insight will deepen understandings of each sub-culture from within and how knowledge differences emerge.

One widely used method for analysis in structural mechanics is the Finite Element Method Analysis (FEM analysis), used for dynamic stressed construction components. As Moaveni notes: '*The finite element method is a numerical procedure that can be applied to obtain solutions to a variety of problems in engineering. Steady, linear, or nonlinear problems in stress analysis ... may be analyzed*' (2003, p. 6). This means that a problem

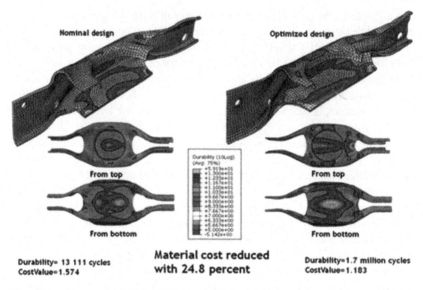

Fig. 5.1 Illustration of the FEM analysis in an imagined piece (http://www.javelin-tech.com/main/images/screenshots/simulation_designer1_lg.jpg, accessed 4 May 2011)

is divided into nodes and elements that split the global piece for analysis into small parts or elements. Each element is assumed to have a shape function in order to have a representation for its physical behavior. An equation is then developed for every element. The next step is to assemble every equation for every element, and then construct the global piece mathematically. This is done in the global stiffness matrix. Boundary conditions, such as the initial condition and loads, are then considered (Moaveni, 2003). By using computer power to calculate the different equations, how the dynamic forces affect an object can be seen visually (Fig. 5.1):

Different colors can indicate different stress levels inflicted on the object which means changes in the global piece can be simulated and differences in stress levels illustrated. FEM is a powerful tool for technological design as failure at this relatively early stage in the product-development phase can have severe consequences later.[2] Primarily, it remains of interest to ask how this powerful tool is used to build knowledge. One could take a scale with theoretical knowledge base at the one end, and practical/experience base at the other. The combination between experience from actual production problems and testing, and the theoretical knowledge about mechanical and material science is essential for a good simulation.

An FEM analysis without practical experience and physical tests has little value. When talking with and interviewing some developers about FEM analysis, a picture of two archetypes of FEM analysts emerged (T1 and T2). It was the way they worked with the tool and the way they argued that set them apart. They create knowledge differently by how they trust their tools and how they argument for their findings.

T1 Its members are very familiar with the stiffness matrix and mathematical equation building, and have spent years building understanding and intuition of the particular part/piece that is produced (practical experience). The material, in question, has always been aluminum alloy. In their heads, they can calculate—or 'see' as they say—roughly 100 elements. In addition, every element they 'see' is strategically placed, while other places have almost no elements. They only calculate the places that they know from experience are significant stress levels, thus using their experience to validate the results coming from the computer simulation.

T2 Its members use computer power and trust modern software for calculations. They can do much more in less time, but there is always the risk of a fault in the positioning of the nodes and elements, and not having enough elements in strategic places. The work is divided into parts that a team solves according to established routines, with as many as 20 people working on a particular part. Nevertheless, this represents a problem, as one developer commented: '*You have so much trust in the process itself that you forget to ask questions regarding the input loads, etc.*'

Some developers in the T2 group expressed the desire to acquire more insight into the stiffness matrix and equations, which is the knowledge type of the T1 group. Interestingly, no one in the T1 group expressed such a strong desire to obtain insight into the computer programs and simulation tools. All of them said it was important, but this was taken care of by the 'younger generation.' Thus, the two groups seemingly fall into an age dimension. However, it is not that simple. Regardless of group, most of the developers mentioned that the maturity of the product should be analyzed. With mature products, the challenge is to see a connection to the production and forming processes, and streamline everything for serial production which is a matter of combining and editing a knowledge type. Less mature products generate much new knowledge that must be verified and checked. At C6, people who fall into the T1 group do most of the more radical innovations. It seems that they have a reflective way of addressing a problem as one developer commented: '*Xx is a person who reflects and asks questions about the fundamentals.*' Asking what he meant about fundamentals, he replied: '*FEM analysis has a fundamental assumption that a material is homogeneous.*' A quick tour into material science reveals that an alloy consists of granulation and impurities that affect its characteristics in ways the FEM analysis does not consider. Another developer said: '*there is a difference between a new understanding and creating new knowledge.*' This meant that understanding is more individual, such as learning a new combination of existing knowledge. Attaining new knowledge is about exploring an entirely new territory that no one in the organization has seen before. Seemingly, the more reflective and less detailed T1 group has an easier route for creating new knowledge. T1 group could receive or establish an idea, and thereafter want to test it, creating an arena of ideas and shared problems where 'trial and error' knowledge dominated. This group had spent years building intuition of the particular part in a practical approach, while the T2 group used words such as robustness and variation a lot, meaning that they strongly believed in designing products and production processes in a way that minimized variations in forms of continuous flow in production and the quality is acceptable. T2 group trusted the answers the computers gave and built their understanding on this. T1 group, however, believed that they can sort this out at a later stage. These archetypes are of course simplifications, only serving as ways of explaining differences. However, the two groups' approaches to knowledge-creation show that there are no unified ways of creating it, even in the same area of expertise. In addition, they acted differently in projects. Hence, understanding how knowledge is created can help to verify the correctness of the results of work and how individuals can be motivated.

THE VOICE OF THE CUSTOMER

Customer demands are hugely important to many actors in the organization. Especially, newcomers to the Raufoss cluster will hear this a lot as nearly every change is explained by new or changed demands from the customer. The research team wanted to investigate this voice of the customer. From Survey #1 we found traces of intense communication with the customer (Fig. 5.2).

Over 70 percent answered that they have at least weekly contact and dialogue with their counterpart customer to which the deeper understanding of

Fig. 5.2 Customer
communication

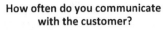

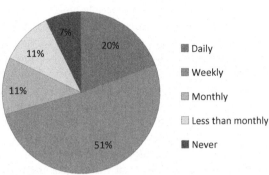

Fig. 5.3 A simplified model of the social network in the Swedish car manufacturer project

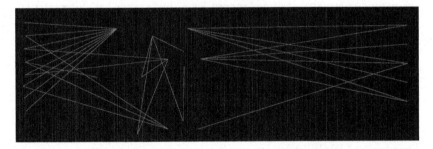

cultural factors regarding intense communication can elaborate on. Intense dialogue creates a paradox as customer demands and specification come in the form of whole quality and project management systems which require a huge amount of documentation. Therefore, there is perhaps no wonder there is intense communication as the actors communicate via phone or in person with the customer side. The feeling was that even though many personal interactions occurred, the intensity was not quite at the level shown in the survey. Investigating it further, the research team conducted a networking survey by asking some of the project members to write down who they talked to in the Swedish car manufacturer project. However, the results contradicted Survey #1 (see Fig. 5.3).

C6 Quality Assurance (QA) is the quality manager and C6 Finite-Element Analysis (FEA) is the manager-in-charge of the FEM analysis. As Fig. 5.3 shows, there are only three people in direct contact with their counterparts at the Swedish car manufacturer. The project leader had the most contacts and most dialogue goes through him. Interviewing the developers with personal customer contacts strengthens this impression. The project members do have contact with their counterparts, but it is mostly during meetings that the project leader sets up and actively participates in. Sitting in such meetings, the research team noticed that the members (represented in the figure as C6a to C6i) were more or less silent unless their opinions were called for. The project leader, C6 QA, or C6 FEA did most of the talking. Further, they had informal conversations with the Swedish car manufacturer between meetings. None of the project members said that they had such conversations. However, the communication between C6 and the Swedish car manufacturer is still at an intense level, but somewhat different than Survey #1 indicated. To understand this intense communication, Flynn's (2009) research into customer understanding at Microsoft will be used as a guide. In addition, we need to understand the difference between the two companies in their work toward the customer.

Working with the Customer

C3 worked with important customers such as Audi/VW, Ford,[3] GM, Daimler, and BMW by having resident engineers onsite at the customers' location. Having resident engineers secures a closeness to the development departments there and served as both an early warning system and consulting service. C6 had discussed such a system of resident engineers but decided on a system of product managers located at Raufoss. These product managers have the responsibility for a product from the early stages of the development project, to the serial production and the product's end-of-life. This approach secures a continuum and one contact point for one platform. It also places product characteristics and quality up front.

These two different ways of serving the customer cannot explain why the research team found traces of intense customer communication on a broad scale in Survey #1. However, people in both companies identified themselves with the customer and claimed to represent their needs at all times. This is parallel to the developers at Microsoft by suggesting 'my customer' is different in line with what Flynn's (2009) study concluded which therefore justifies communication. Therefore, it leads us to ask: Can this notion of customer communication be a motivating factor that can somehow be exaggerated?

Motivation Factor

A demanding customer is often mentioned as the driving force of development which is certainly both tacitly and explicitly understood at Raufoss. An automobile manufacturer's demands take the form of product characteristics, price, and weight, with one interviewee commenting: '*The customer guides us 100 percent. The customer is the motivator for working with improvements. We are not Bosch, which every manufacturer is dependent on; we need to do what the customer wants us to do to improve.*' This statement clearly shows a strong connection and identification toward the customer. However, what kinds of customer demands trigger motivation for working with improvements were unclear. The customer sets the goals for improvement in, for example, the lifespan of a product demanding a price reduction at 5 percent per year; an auto manufacturer will motivate the tier structure to improve continuously its production and development process. Contractual motivation factors, such as a yearly price reduction, are very common in the industry, although the customer also provokes them to take risks in development. In addition, for a company located in a small Norwegian town, motivation is also in line with survival as an existential motivation which is difficult to live with over time, and can wear people down. Notably, whenever we talked to the product developers about the customer demands there was 'fire' in their eyes and excitement in their voices.

Response Time and Validation

Raufoss' milieu strongly believes that a fast response time is something that they are better at than their competitors. This is manifested not only in the storytelling of a crisis, but also in the everyday life of product development. As one developer told us: '*If a customer does not get a test right or has another failure, they know they can call us and a new improved part is underway ... a quick response time settles and calms the customer. It is quite brilliant!*' This is not something that is meant to serve the customer on a business level, but rather on a more personal level, '*because the people working on the other side [our comment: the customer] also want to have peace and quiet in their everyday work.*' There is an understanding of everyday life on a personal basis, as well as a technological understanding that when something goes wrong which can help bring the people on both sides closer. Understanding that they both live under demanding job conditions, transparent explanations to people with similar competencies when something goes wrong are easier than to someone working in sales. On this individual level, similar competencies and function are characterized as good and the source of the demand or people with other competences and function are bad for making such demands.

Due to the flat and informal organizational structures of the companies located at Raufoss, decisions can easily be made in the hallway or by one employee walking into his superior's office, as it is common for the office door to always be open. However, a developer also identified himself with the known achievements of a particular person with regard to a customer and brought the statement to an individual level. Here again, the parallel to Microsoft can be seen as the common practice of referring to Bill Gates' achievement of changing the way people work (Flynn, 2009). We understand this parallel as saying: '*Little me can play an important part even for the big Customer or OEM.*'

One interesting aspect of response time came in a discussion with a product manager at C6. He said that he had solved some problems very quickly, and in doing so, he thought he had done a great job for the customer. Even so, the customer opposed him and asked him to go deeper into the problem. This customer wanted to wait two or three days and then receive an explanation that dealt with the root cause. Such an approach is becoming more and more common. Having identified what seems to be the root cause and putting forward an action plan for how to deal with this problem is now becoming increasingly accepted as the pattern to follow. The validating power ultimately sits with the customer, as they have their tests and specifications that the product must satisfy.

Relationships and Patience: Corrective Factor

The corrective factor of relationships and patience show how the voice of the customer serves as a corrective factor. We have already seen how understanding is considered on the individual everyday working level, in which a fault can be rectified by a very quick response time and is something that 'saves the day.' However, making a solid, robust product that meets the requirements and specifications of the customer is more common. Making things right is the overall goal for the development team. If a customer gets the impression that a fault is under investigation and a plan has been made to determine the root cause, the customer is more patient. As such, it was interesting for the research team to investigate why Raufoss companies had a low success rate with Japanese car manufacturers. Traditionally, the Japanese companies have been thought of as having the best quality products that never break down. Surely, having a Japanese customer would be a great asset for a small Norwegian parts manufacturer involved in global competition. Taking this thought to the marketing manager at C3, he told us that even though they have good contacts with companies such as Toyota, Honda, and Nissan, C3 cannot be patient enough to manifest these contacts into sales. Japanese companies are very long-term minded, and demand a personal and social relationship with their suppliers. Being present in Japan is definitely advantageous he told us, yet in the Norwegian tradition, the building of customer relations over many years before a contract is signed is not acceptable. C6 managed to get a contract with one Japanese car manufacturer, but the product manager also points that a patient attitude is required.

Looking at a more common customer such as the German car manufacturer, there is trust between the developers at both firms. On the company level, this manifests itself by lower, less rigid quality control. The quality inspector at the German manufacturer in charge of checking C3 has said that he does not spend much time doing so, and the developers at C3 in charge of products to that customer explained that this trust is institutional, built on serving the customer's needs over many years. The developers have shown that they know what they are doing whereby technological expertise and quick response times on important requests are mentioned as the underlying explanation, with a noticeably slacker, informal development environment in ongoing projects as the result. One senior developer summarized how they worked and felt: '*We all live and breathe with the problems; problem-solving is our (our addition: professional) life.*' Asking what he meant about 'we,' he replayed product-development department. In addition, problems were related to activities and projects in there and he mentioned the problems as if they were common knowledge understood by everybody—the 'we.' Ambiguity over customer demands is always referred to the others; the industrializations, or operations, named 'they.' When variations in quality were found, a task group was formed in the capable hands of the developer and a quick solution was found, thereby solving the problem. If the problem reoccurred, a new quick fix was implemented which frustrated the operators. Instead of fixing the root cause, symptoms were fixed and this was against the continuous improvement thinking of operations. However, it complied more with the focus of satisfying the customer.

Sense-Making of the Development Process and Systems

Western understanding and sense-making is built on rationality with chance and probability as important components of this reasoning. However, when accidents happen and involve those close to us, it can be difficult to reason in this way. Many tend to claim that God is punishing us, and rational thought is put aside. Evans-Pritchard and Gillies (1976) first discovered this during a visit to a native tribe in Africa. Termites ate a post holding up scaffolding, it fell and killed a man. The tribe called it witchcraft. Evans-Pritchard and Gillies tried reasoning with them about the termites causing the accident and that there was no witchcraft involved. The answer was that evidently they saw the damage made by termites, but that did not explain why the scaffold fell on that man on that day, and therefore they were right. We claim to accept the concept of probability and chance, but in times of grief or pressure we find other explanations. This discovery was important because it illustrated a failure in our intellectual system. The book by Kushner (1981), *When Bad Things Happen to Good People*, deals with this failure and how we tackle such situations. People try to make sense of the situation even when there is no sense. It is easy to explain accidents due to changes and incidents. However, if the accident happens to someone close to us this rational claim can be replaced with other explanations.

The need of having an explanation for bad things happening to us exists. In the Kushner case, it was his son's death due to 'progeria,' a rapid aging disease. Being a rabbi in the local community, he saw himself and his work as something good. By strongly believing that God is somewhat of a strict fatherly figure punishing bad people for doing bad things, the central question therefore became: '*why do bad things happen to good people?*' The question triggers a form of sense-making of a situation that does not make sense. We see this, although in a different scale, in companies.

People working in a product-development department deal with lots of pressure and contradictory demands. They are subject to many forces that are beside or beyond their control, which makes everyday work difficult and can change the agenda for what is done daily. In many ways, it can be thought of as dealing with a scaled-down version of the existential crisis.

To survive in such a chaotic and changeable environment, the developers need to make some sort of sense of their situation, even if it makes no sense. Making sense of the situation is essential for people's motivation, sanity, and self-image. It is essential for the developers to continue working under such circumstances. Therefore, it is important to understand how product developers make sense of their environments and job situations. It is the basis of their identity as working professionals in a truly global industry. Another important point is that they cannot change this difficult work situation as it is part of 'life.' Adding to this, much of the research was conducted in times of existential crisis where customers went bankrupt and the entire financial system nearly collapsed. The sense-making process for the developers was made easier by these external factors as such issues contributed to various reflections in the developers' mind-sets.

When Weick (1995) introduced sense-making as a theoretical analytic tool, he coined the individual's effort to place order in a chaos called reality. Klemsdal (2008, p. 87) defined—based on Weick—sense-making as:

> ... a process that is evoked when we are interrupted in our ongoing daily activities by our expectations not being met; it is about making sense of a situation, an event, or a phenomenon that is new to us and experienced as ambiguous.

At C6, sense-making regards how the developers understood their situations and coped with the time pressure and contradictory demands. Weick has a section on the future of sense-making where he wrote organizational culture is about encouraging shared experience (1995, pp. 188–189). Here, he argues for shared meaning being based on shared experience whereby '*[p]eople construct shared meaning for a shared experience*' (ibid., p. 189) which gives us two things. First, sense-making, or shared meaning in this case, is an activity that is done retrospectively. Second, shared meaning is an interpretation of an experience, which is also an action. Thereby, sense-making broadly speaks about analyzing two components—action and interpretation.

The previous sections have painted a picture of asymmetric and complex relationships between OEM and supplier. In addition, the developers' everyday life seemed to be dominated by high stress levels and contradictory demands from a demanding customer. The important question is how they cope with this and make sense of their environment. It is hard to see from the stories how employees can have routines, coherent structures, and orderly processes that make sense. We will argue that the key of understanding how sense-making is conducted lies hidden in the following various parameters: the local community, the motivation to be at the forefront of engineering and material science, the dialogue with counterparts at the customer's office, and the quality and project management systems' functions.

The local environment consists of two small towns that have experienced many crises and unemployment, but still manage to 'ride the storm' time after time. In Norway, the word 'dugnad'[4] means doing something for the collective well-being without pay. It is deeply rooted and in small communities where it becomes obvious who contributes, especially appropriate in times of crisis. However, 'dugnad' is something social, associated with spare time activities, as well as related to work where often employees hear that they need to 'roll up their sleeves and make an extra effort' for the company. In addition, performing 'dugnad' for the company also means securing local jobs and thereby doing it for the local community. However, although 'dugnad' is without initial pay, it is an important aspect for the following annual salary negotiations. Thus, this goes some way to explain why developers take on crises such as the Christmas and Easter actions, but not how they cope with continuous pressure and changes.

Motivations need explanation through an illustrative story via the lengthy interview with the developer of the Italian car manufacturer incident. One reason for this lengthy interview was his passion for engineering and material science. When the interview was agreed, he thought of the researcher as an economist with no technological interest. However, during the interview, as he commented some months later, he became aware that the researcher was indeed technologically interested and into production processes and therefore he offered lengthy explanations of every little detail; not only for the Italian car manufacturer incident, but for the whole development process and the material properties of the exact aluminum alloy used. In addition, he was sidetracked telling the researcher about a lecture he gave for an OEM. Initially, he thought he was invited to present the properties of different aluminum alloys used in suspension parts and that the interest in it could be no greater than five people. However, when he arrived at the OEM's headquarters it turned out that an auditorium of over 100 people formed the audience. Moreover, he continued to talk the researcher through the whole lecture, and as he did, the 'fire' in his eyes and the excitement in his voice grew. This had been a very special experience for him, and still (then) motivated him. In other words, the challenge can stimulate and motivate the developer instead of being defeated by it. Others have also experienced giving lectures to the customer. One developer said that he had just been to a Teardown,[5] which was motivational for both the individual and organization because they participated in collecting and gathering knowledge that the advanced customer requested. Winning contracts against cheaper steel parts is taken as evidence that they are in the forefront of engineering and material science. This explains, to some degree, the interpretations that in the minds of the developer it makes sense to have a demanding customer. However, if the conditions are bad then it is difficult to stay motivated from day-to-day.

DIALOGUE AND SENSE-MAKING

As previously commented, there is intense dialogue between people working at development department at C6 and its OEM counterpart where daily or weekly conversations are important parts of the sense-making process, together with the quality and project management systems. First, speaking with the counterpart on a regular basis is a huge motivational factor that C6 and C3's developers all mentioned during interviews. Sitting in on some of these conversations, niceties were kept to a minimum as the participants went—more or less—straight to the technological subject that was in focus, explaining and making sense of the challenges that were currently present. The conversation was detailed and focused. It took the research team some time to figure out how they could so quickly start talking about very detailed stuff and immediately understand each other. The clue to answer this came from the quality expert in the research team. Even though each OEM has its own quality system, the systems are built from the same platform. Ford, GM, and Chrysler started the Automotive Industry Action Group (AIAG) in 1982 to make a framework and develop recommendations for quality improvements. It resulted in the framework of Advanced Product Quality Planning, known as APQP in the automotive industry—the 'father' of all the American automakers quality systems and to some degree the European ISO standards. The quality expert called the automakers own quality systems as dialects of the same. The basis, APQP, includes four major manuals (FMEA, Statistical process control, measurement systems analysis, and production part approval process). Furthermore, APQP monitors 23 major topics from

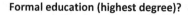

Formal education (highest degree)?

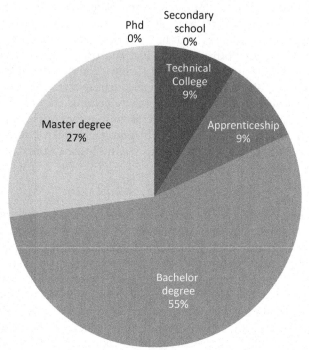

Fig. 5.4   Formal education

cradle to grave for a product, or car in this case. Learning APQP takes years. However, it provides the developers with a common language similar to the doctors' usage of Latin in their profession. All developers at C6 were well educated, experienced, and therefore spoke this language fluently (see Figs. 5.4 and 5.5).

Weekly or daily talks are a way of learning and keeping a continuous sense-making process going. Close contact breaks large amounts of work into manageable pieces. Problems are informally solved before they become issues in the official quality system. Depending on where the project is in the schedule there are either monthly or weekly reports to be handed in to the OEM. Reporting dates and report forms are predefined from the beginning of the project. During a two-year development project,

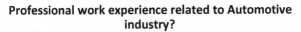

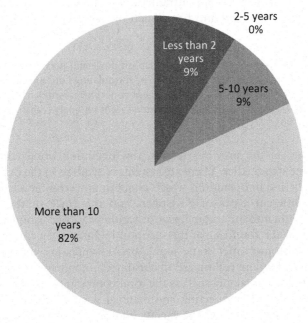

Fig. 5.5 Work experience in automotive industry

it is common to have four to six onsite reviews, where the project representatives from the OEM visit the supplier. In these, the OEM examines
every quality report. After being present at some reviews, the actions were
different. They quickly checked if the forms were filled in but did not go
into detail of what was written. One can think of this as a shortcut, but the
people involved defended the practice. They argued that close collaboration and communication meant that they knew the details. The onsite
review was more of a ritual of checking and filling in an official report than
checking what has been done. The spared time was used to go into mutual
reflections over the technological challenges and progress information to
the overall new car model project. Our reaction was one of surprise at how
easily the onsite review was conducted, and how this practice was not in
accordance to the rules in the quality system. However, the time usage and
reflections were helpful, allowing the project to go forward.

CONCLUSION: ORGANIZATIONAL CULTURE

In this chapter of internal contradictions in business, Martin's (1992) perspective is amplified and broadened by using Geertz's definition of religion:

> a system of symbols which acts to establish powerful, pervasive, and long-lasting moods and motivations in men by formulating conceptions of a general order of existence and clothing these conceptions with such an aura of factuality that the moods and motivations seem uniquely realistic. (Geertz, 1973, p. 90)

Building on the previous stories, this definition brings the cultural analysis one step further. There are systems of symbols in the development department and in operations which establish powerful moods and motivations. Different types of developers and the voice of the customer provide insight into the argument as the various ways of creating knowledge and being at the forefront of this creation by intensively communicating with the customer offer some highlights. Formulating conceptions, an aura of factuality, and realism are all illustrated in the sense-making activity which is hidden in factors such as the local community, motivations to be at the forefront of engineering and material sciences, the dialogue with customer counterpart, and the quality and project management systems established.

Overall, such broadening and amplification of the differentiated culture dimension contributes to cultural theory. In addition, this points toward the need for different management roles in order to keep such a differentiated company culture together to achieve performance that maintains and develops competitive advantages, enabling the companies to compete on a global market. Chapter 7 extends this further by investigating the managerial aspects involved.

NOTES

1. 'Dugnad' is a Norwegian word for volunteer work or means doing something for the collective well-being without pay—will be elaborated further later in the book.
2. The consequences can be production tools that break, a failure in tests, etc.
3. NE was still owned by Ford when the interview in C3 was conducted.
4. 'Dugnad' is discussed further in the facilitative management chapter.

5. Teardown is when an OEM takes one of the competitors' cars and disassembles it. In this way, they can analyze the parts and find out how it is produced. It is regarded as an acknowledgement of one's competence to participate in this.

REFERENCES

Evans-Pritchard, E. E., & Gillies, E. (1976). *Witchcraft, oracles, and magic among the Azande.* Oxford: Oxford University Press.

Flynn, D. K. (2009). "My customers are different!" Identity, difference, and the political economy of design. In M. Cefkin (Ed.), *Ethnography and the corporate encounter: Reflections on research in and of corporations.* New York: Berghahn Books.

Geertz, C. (1973). *The interpretation of cultures.* New York: Basic Books.

Klemsdal, L. (2008). *Making sense of "the new way of organizing": Managing the micro processes of (planned) change in a municipality* (Vol. 2008:300). Trondheim: Norges teknisk-naturvitenskapelige universitet.

Kushner, H. S. (1981). *When bad things happen to good people.* New York: Schocken Books.

Martin, J. (1992). *Cultures in organizations: Three perspectives.* New York: Oxford University Press.

Moaveni, S. (2003). *Finite element analysis: Theory and application with ANSYS.* Upper Saddle River, NJ: Pearson Education.

Weick, K. E. (1995). *Sensemaking in organizations.* London: Sage.

CHAPTER 6

Facilitative Management

Abstract Many of the broad managerial trends, that is, the Lean tradition, have a strong focus on operations at the production line level and tend to overemphasize explicit knowledge. This chapter demonstrates, based on empirical evidence from a global car part producer, the importance and the strength of tacit knowledge components as value-creation ingredients. The discussion relates to the old controversy between Ohno and Nemoto (the father of Toyota Production System and the first quality director at Toyota) whereby the former posed that actual quality awareness was in the minds of the operators as opposed to the explicit forms of instructions and check-lists which typically are the focus of production managers.

Introduction

This chapter focuses on the managerial aspects of leading a modern manufacturing company in a global competitive environment. It starts with the macro foundations of Norwegian work-life that contradict the common argument that competitive advantage suffers with high labor costs. In addition, it describes the 'dugnad' spirit in relationships with sense-making. Such macro foundations are not unique to Norway, rather a smart leader knows how to tap into these societal foundations for corporate benefit by enacting on them. In addition, a description of

© The Author(s) 2018
H. Holtskog et al., *Learning Factories*, Palgrave Studies in
Democracy, Innovation, and Entrepreneurship for Growth,
https://doi.org/10.1007/978-3-319-41887-2_6

the individual's increased vulnerability by the general personalization of work and working conditions is offered. The foundations and personalization tendencies therefore create a backdrop describing facilitative management.

Facilitative management is the realization of social partnership in the organization which allows the differentiated cultures to work together. It takes on a different leadership approach than control. Facilitative management is about enabling the organization to find good solutions for problems. Hirschhorn (1997) argues for a culture of openness and its implications on the leadership role or facilitative management. Five stories investigate such culture and leadership roles. First, a story of the new project manager with a North-European car manufacturer deals with the leadership challenges in existential difficult times. The story investigates the foundation for authority in a matrix organization. Second, we investigate how a new foreign CEO understood his position and gradually changed his leadership style. Third, the focus turns toward the accountant's leadership role where relying on numbers generated in the financial statements produces 'management by number.' However, we argue for a more insightful use of numbers directly linked to the actual activity and value-creation processes, or cost management which broadens the classical discussion around Activity-Based Costs (ABC), and is similar to the argument of why accountability-based quality control does not produce quality. Fourth, managing operations is important, and the section starts with a critique of the Lean tradition before picking up the story of task teams (or task force) and broadening this to the leader's role. Finally, the chapter looks at the relationship between the OEM and supplier from a leader's viewpoint before ending by describing general aspects of facilitative management and the two general focuses: partnership orchestration and pivoting problems.

Macro Foundation in Norwegian Work-Life: Company Impact

To truly understand how work-life operates in the companies at Raufoss, it is important to provide insight into how Norwegian work-life operates. It is different from, for example, the American system where most of the theories used in this thesis originated from. As mentioned in Chaps. 2 and 3, the Norwegian model and work-life research have together gone through different phases resulting in different agreements and legislations.

However, the impact on the companies is important to understand when we look at their leadership.

The Working Environmental Act is a cornerstone in the work-life collaboration in Norway, but this is not detailed here as many other countries now have similar legislations. What is special and needs to be explained is the partnership between the unions, owner's confederation, and the government. Generally, the foundation for wages is centrally set on a regular basis followed by local additions negotiated in every company. The central negotiation for wage regulation follows functions and branches. One central principle is that frontline branches' negotiations are first, setting the standard for the others. By frontline branches we mean, for example, manufacturing and processing industries that compete in the global market. The rationality behind this is to set a norm that maintains the competitiveness of these branches where governmental organizations or other domestic branches cannot drive up wages which would go into an inflation spiral that could damage the frontline companies. Another argument is to decrease the impact of the oil and gas industry on the economy due to it being a large supplier which could cause Norwegian wages to significantly increase more. The principle of frontline branches requires collaboration between the parties and some agreed guidelines to follow. One such guideline is the regulation of peace and conflict times. Peacetime, broadly speaking, is the time between these negotiations. Conflict time is during the negotiations and halting. Under certain circumstances and with messages to the other party, strikes or lockouts can be used as power tools. The design of this system is to make the work-life predictable and not hurt the vulnerable export industry. The parties respect these guidelines and often turn to the government for help when negotiations halt. Instead of a costly conflict, it can be resolved by a forced wage setting and the government as the intervening agent in a conflict when life and safety are at risk.

Social welfare in Norway began four decades ago to ensure there was no poverty, as well as creating equal opportunities, and solidarity. In the beginning, the focus was on poverty fighting, and over time, the latter two have increasingly come into focus. Although this topic is beyond the scope of this book, it is important to understand that equal opportunity in Norway means that everyone can receive government loans for education at low interest rates with no security as one example. It therefore means that it is relatively cheap to obtain higher education. Consequently, the population is becoming more educated, and companies are believed to benefit from this over time. Solidarity means unemployment wages are paid by the government which creates some security. However, there are strings attached as jobseekers need to be actively applying for new jobs or undergoing requalification programs for other employment types. The general belief is that these mechanisms in Norwegian work-life both form the solid foundation for security and benefit the companies. Secure employees work better and are self-thinkers. However, employees in a redundancy situation risk financial ruin, feel insecure, and perhaps tend to follow orders. Although in Norway, there are strict regulations about layoffs regarding regulations and the principle of seniority which means the young are at greater risk. This follows the rational argument that senior workers have valuable experience for the company and are less attractive for entirely new jobs, in addition to their length of time serving the company.

However, Norway is not a haven for social democrats. The national agreement between the work-life parties is under stress for many reasons. First, Norway is part of the global community and its companies compete on the global arena. Second, many of the companies are no longer Norwegian owned but part of larger multinational enterprises. Third, huge natural resources of oil and gas obtain high profits thereby accelerate salaries. However, economically, natural resources have played a significant role in changing the economic structure. The oil and gas industry has driven labor wages up with higher domestic demands for higher wages and all of these social agreements and democratic arrangements have produced a national cost level that is among the highest in the world (see Table 6.1). Finally, there are political reasons, such as the right wing gaining momentum in Norwegian politics, accelerating public social costs, and so on.

As Table 6.1 shows, the Nordic countries have high labor costs with an average of 125 compared to the G7 countries of 108. Europe stands at 112. On the top, Norway is at 143 (in 2012 it reached 148). The figures prove the high cost levels and more precisely the high cost of labor. Having this and remaining competitive on the global automotive market is difficult. The answer at Raufoss is highly automated production lines[1] with very few operators.

The picture shows people working with assembly details that machines cannot do. Highly automated lines do not have people working intensively on the shop floor.

Table 6.1 Organization for Economic Co-operation and Development (OECD) unit labor costs

Country	2011
Norway	143
Iceland	140
Finland	118
Denmark	118
Sweden	107
United Kingdom	117
Germany	104
France	112
United States	112
Japan	93
G7	108
OECD—Europe	112
OECD—Total	110

http://stats.oecd.org/Index.aspx?DatasetCode=ULC_ ANN—these are the numbers at the same time as the survey was conducted. No significant change in the number for the Nordic countries after this. They still have relatively high labor cost

Here, workers are not present on the shop floor unless something is wrong, for inspection purposes or maintenance. When a leader wants to talk to the worker, he would find them in control rooms overlooking the production lines. In a sense, the workers are managers themselves as they manage machines. Normally, a worker has the responsibility of several machines. These production lines require huge investments in equipment. The price of equipment is, more or less, the same all over the world, and the equipment reduces the need for workers to a minimum, thereby cutting labor costs. However, the skill level of the workforce enhances such production. This is the essence of the explanation managers make when they try to explain why they are competitively producing parts for a global market. The managers that we talked to have also explained that the production is very efficient compared to what they see elsewhere. Putting it all together from the former discussions, demanding customers, annually decreasing sales prices, high labor costs, and high takt production set the stage for a stressful working environment. However, the social partnership in the society with democratic processes motivates and informs people about possibilities, challenges, and limitations in the society and companies, as well as forms social partnership within. In such partnership, volunteerism tends to be present. A unified understanding of the current situation and the demand for the future eases the process of creating common goals. It creates a sense of internal solidarity.

At the end of Chap. 5 concerning internal contradictions, how developers make sense of this stressful environment was explained. To secure the workplace in times of crisis, unpaid work helps the local community (discussed by the Norwegian word of 'dugnad'). In addition, as a member of the community, the demand is to participate in this. In some senses, it is a fight for the community that benefits the company. This fight is not unique to Norway and we can see similarities in many countries with social democratic traditions. In cooperative companies, this spirit is part of the fundament (Greenwood & González Santos, 1992). However, a smart leader knows how to tap into such solidarity and enact upon it.

Overall, these selected factors are macro foundations for the companies, but we have also tried to highlight the benefits for the companies and thereby exemplify a way of management thinking. Now it is time to leave these macro foundations and concentrate on the companies themselves.

PERSONALIZATION AND QUALITY/MANAGEMENT SYSTEM

Before going into the leadership aspects, it is important to look at the general working conditions for employees in modern industry. With the development of different systems and management logic over recent decades, work—even in operations—has become more individualized. Quality systems require signatures on different forms, tracing products down to each stage in production, as well as the increased possibility of output supervision at each workstation and so on. These all contribute to the possibility of measuring each individual's performance. The Lean production tradition advocates teamwork; however, it too can measure individual performance. In the quest of perfection and quality, Ohno (the 'father' of the Toyota Production System) told each operator that any incoming parts with quality issues should be sent out of the production line. The manager can see where faulty parts are sent out and go upstream to find the problems. Any attempts to fix faults were simply not permitted because if the operators did so, they would hide unsatisfactory processes upstream (Ohno, 1988; Shimokawa & Fujimoto, 2010). We find this contradictory to the team work effort and method because sending items out of the line will show where the fault occurred, which may create scapegoats for the 'problem.' It does, however, allow constraints in the production flow to be discovered so that it can be improved. Nevertheless, the manner in which the flow is improved is the main point. In a Tayloristic tradition or learning model O-I, certain people analyze the situation and the result is brought back to the problem site, while O-II model will include inquiry and reflection stage with the stakeholders, where the solutions are products of the inquiry from the stage which makes a difference.

There is a tendency to measure and identify individual effort for value-creation in companies today (Ghoshal & Bartlett, 1997) by developing new ways of rewarding the individual employee (Foss, Pedersen, Pyndt, & Schultz, 2012). This individualization or personalization leads to employee vulnerability. In a product-development project with a small number of people, this is especially true. However, saying this is not the same as saying it is something bad. Ingvaldsen, Holtskog, and Ringen (2013) found that employees in the production line want to be seen as individuals and require improved feedback from management observing their performance. The important difference between surveillance and this desire for feedback lays hidden in the execution of the leadership role. An alternative to measuring individual performance is to use it as an input to a reflection phase. However, the presence of openness in the organizational environment is mandatory and must go both ways (Hirschhorn, 1997). Therefore, it is natural to take a closer look at the leadership role and authority in such culture of openness. In openness, the fragile foundation for collaboration is important to understand as well as the impact of structure.

FOUNDATION OF AUTHORITY

The third power tradition agrees with the two other identified ones that a leader needs to have some control over decision-making and agenda setting. Issues and potential issues are just as important (Lukes, 2005).

Going back to the project with a North-European car manufacturer at C6, the project leader displayed the foundations for leadership extremely well. This was his first project as leader, but he had had long experience with other similar projects as both worker and developer. He had a master's degree in mechanical engineering. Rather than taking tools from the management and quality system, he introduced what he called an 'issue list' as a simple list of what to do, who is responsible for the activity, and when it should be finished or 'closed.' This 'new invention' was welcomed by the project members as a simplification of the car manufacturer's progress reports. It resulted in saved time and fewer project meetings. Everyone could see what everyone needed to do until the next meeting.

However, eventually people lagged behind in their work which resulted in new closing dates. Gradually, this became irritating for people working late to meet them as during the project meetings, the leader did not comment when he changed the dates. Workers could sense no reaction from him at all when they told him they could not reach the original deadline.

Over time, the quality manager as the main contact person in the company called and asked if we could help bring up this issue with the project leader. He was afraid that the project would not meet its required deadline which is seen as a disaster in the automotive industry. Specifically, Start of Production (SOP) date is a fixed date to which every subcontractor or supplier starts the delivery of parts to the new model for assembly. Everything should be on time at the correct quality and quantity according to the just-in-time principle. The concern of the quality manager in not meeting the SOP date resulted in a meeting between the quality manager, the project leader, and one of the researchers during which the project leader was very honest and open. He listened to what the quality manager had to say, but defended his use of the issue list and meant that the project was on track. Gradually, another underlying issue of the quality manager's concern emerged, the extra work the issue list meant for him. He had to 'translate' the issue list into the official documents of the customer. After we figured out how this should be done, the researcher brought in the frustrations from the project workers who worked hard to meet deadlines or closing dates while others just kept receiving new dates. This frustration was something the project leader had not thought about because—as he said—there are good reasons for changing the closing dates of some activities. After this, he reflected that he had not specifically communicated the reasons for changing dates. Often this came about before the meetings. Many project members visited his office between meetings, discussing extended deadlines and problems of a more serious nature. Overall, what we had was informal project work documentation in the form of issue lists and informal meeting structures. Some important decision-making was informal and did not follow the formal structure, systems, and meetings, although were emphasized and documented in formal systems and meetings.

A few days later, the project leader met us for another discussion about the project's leadership. He had made some personal reflections. The first action he wanted was to better inform everyone in the official project meeting about the extended deadlines. This was good, but led us to question why it had not previously been done. He said he did not want people to lose face in front of the others. In addition, most of the time there were really good reasons for extending the deadline. This corresponded well with the interviewed project members who all admired his competence and thought of him as a great person. His competence was such that he immediately understood a problem when it was described to him. Feelings of accomplishment were also common. The project manager's behavior was of a quiet nature, but he showed real interest in everyone's work and progress. He always took time to talk with his employees and praise others' accomplishments when groups were gathered. Telling him this made him think about his leadership role. He asked if he listened too much and favored some before others. However, this was not what the essence of the interviews was with the project members. They liked that he listened and made time, but they missed clear closing dates and sometimes a leader's clear commands. Clear commands included more strict closing dates because every activity is dependent on others, and one delay risks delaying the sequential activities. We asked project members why they thought the project leader did not issue clear commands and nearly all of them said that he was a nice person and it was not in his nature. Since the project leader had a calm and gentle personality, he thought that some disagreements between members resolved themselves, and this thought irritated some who felt it was the leader's job to solve disagreements. In general, the members' hidden argument was that they started questioning the project leader's ability to lead. One member more openly said: '*remember there are wolves [he pointed then to the offices of other project leaders] that will try to take all your time if your main project leader does not watch out.*' This statement also leads to the fact that members were working on more than one project at a time.

Armed with this, we challenged the project leader to be more informative during project meetings and more commanding in the way he told people what to do. He listened and asked a couple of questions to make sure he understood what was meant. Attending the next project meeting, he was much more informative and it was lengthy. However, he still did not give orders. Later, he said that this part felt unnatural to him and he would rather deal with poor performance one-to-one than in a meeting with many people present. We agreed with him realizing that some of the delays were actually due to poor performance and not due to difficulty and complexity. His main concern was to keep up his members' motivation during difficult times which we found sensible.

Thereafter, we received a challenge from the project manager who wanted an efficient way to present and inform project members. The research team worked on several suggestions, and ended up presenting three to the project team. The first regarded an improved checklist that could replace the issue list and was in accordance with customer demands. The reaction from several members was '*oh, another form to learn!*' So, this suggestion was dropped. The second was a little bit challenging by improving the way of working with FMEA,[2] dividing it into three different forms with the general RPNs separated from the specific ones. In this way, the discussions could be more focused and specific on the actual challenges for that particular product or process. The reaction was very positive and a task force involved in FMEA worked out the details based on these initial ideas. Third, we suggested establishing an 'obeya room.'[3] Due to office space issues, however, a movable whiteboard served this purpose. The research team established the suggestion and started hanging up project reports, forms, diagrams, and so on, keeping it up-to-date at the beginning. It stood near the coffee cans between project meetings in the hopes that people would gather around the board and start talking about problems and progress. Before the project meetings, the board was rolled into the meeting room. After a slow start with almost no interest from the project members, the interest began to grow. The informative part in the project meetings went much faster and people said that they were actually better informed regarding the overall picture. However, the 'saved' time was used to discuss more details that interested just a few strong individuals. In addition, the goal of having the board as the center of coffee breaks for discussions did not catch on. Several members, while talking, told us that the whiteboard triggered some discussions, but these discussions quickly changed place into the offices, where more detailed information could be found. Overall, the board was semi-successful as it initiated focused discussions and speed up information exchange, but was never fully adopted by the organizational members. As for the leadership role and ordering issue, the board showed very clearly who had fallen behind. The research team was never able to investigate fully if that had an effect on performance as the board came into the project at a late state. However, the leader was satisfied as it meant that poor performers were no longer an issue. Nevertheless, we cannot take full credit for the board, as the project leader also held personal meetings with his staff. One of the final comments illustrated the leader's maturing: '*he knows now what he wants, but he is still a very nice guy.*' It also shows the foundations on which authority has been built for him such as: deep engineering knowledge; insight into what activities need to be done; solving problems and issues in smaller groups or individually; motivation via performance appraisal; and trusting one's own judgment. Also, his ability to stay firm but cool in heated discussions, knowing that these are learning tools for the participants, was vital.

Changing the Leader's Role: CEO

The change of CEO at C6 was a shock for many. The new CEO made many of the most experienced people go into early retirement, many of whom were heroes in the organization's eyes. He also wanted to terminate C6's involvement in the research project as the company was experiencing huge profit losses and he thought it was best to concentrate on existing procedures and production, before learning and developing new ones. In addition, he believed that the main research dealt with new materials and production techniques. This misconception was clear; people in the development department defended and argued for continuous participation. In a meeting with some of the research team, the CEO agreed to stay with the project, but that the team should focus on only one—the project with a North-European car manufacturer—to help with practical issues. We thought we could manage to combine practical help with investigating how the development department made knowledge. Therefore, we did not see it as a major shift.

The following week when visiting C6, the new CEO's presence was very clear. Everyone sat in their offices and worked. Hallway talk or sitting in each other's offices and discussing important issues was kept to a minimum. The CEO sat behind a closed door. Suddenly, the CEO would walk up and down the hallways in both floors and go back to his office, not talking to anyone and closing the door behind him. It was a very dismal feeling in the office building. A few days later, all employees gathered for a meeting where the new CEO informed about the company his plans and the way forward. After the meeting the atmosphere was a little lighter, people started talking to each other and work went back to a more normalized state. However, the walks up and down the hallways continued for weeks to come. After asking several of the employees how they felt, they all answered that it was a special situation, but they were confident that in collaboration with the new CEO they should be able to 'ride out the storm.'

Some weeks later, we interviewed a key person in the development department. Then suddenly the new CEO came into the meeting room which had glass walls without knocking. He wondered who we were and what we were doing. Upon clearing up this matter, he then wondered why we were interviewing this person as he should not have been working in the North-European car manufacturer project. Not waiting for an answer, he left the room. The developer told us that the new CEO had no idea what people were doing in the organization. Further, he did not understand how they worked and how much work was needed in order to develop a car part. The CEO's former position was head of the alumina profile companies in the same enterprise. Making a new profile was similar to making a new production tool before the new product went into production which is quite different from car parts manufacturing that requires testing, forging, assembly, and so on. The developer, however, was positive about the new CEO but very skeptical of the former who he thought had employed too many, as currently they had half the work force but still managed to produce the same.

After this interview, we arranged our talks in the developers' offices behind closed doors and solid, not glass walls. Nevertheless, everyone we talked to expressed the importance of having stricter rules and leadership in the organization. When we asked what kind of rules, it was difficult to obtain good honest answers. Many pointed to a stricter regime in documenting work hours, lunch breaks, and so on. It seemed, however, that no new rules were actually introduced although obeying the existing ones was emphasized, resulting in a better structure of the working day for many.

Just before the research project started, C6 introduced a new organizational structure with product managers. These managers had the responsibility for a development project product from production to liquidation which continued throughout the research project period. Specifically, it accelerated after the financial crisis as the new CEO made these managers responsible for the product even when it had gone into series-production. He expected them to additionally be part of problem-solving in production. Gradually, the focus was turned to also include production and, interestingly, many old production issues that had originated from development were solved. Therefore, the new CEO certainly contributed to a positive turn.

However, more obvious to the research team was when the CEO stopped his walks up and down the hallway and the office door stayed open. We even saw him sitting and talking friendly to an employee long after lunch should have been finished. Such behavior stood in stark contrast to the beginning. He also earned respect by working very long hours. In sum, his effort in saving the company was beyond expectations. During the first project meeting he attended, the atmosphere was unique. Nobody asked questions or talked unless necessary. Later, he still attended in silence, but the meetings returned to normal with technological discussions and innovative ideas. At the end, he would comment on them as 'good' or 'on the right track.' The middle managers described him as fair and very interested. The research team asked several times for an interview, but he very polity refused. In addition, even the union representative started to say that he was a team player.

From the initial shock of changing the CEO and the insecurity that followed, the new CEO filled his leadership role with surveillance and command. However, he soon found out that it was not the way forward and intelligently changed it to fit the organization's needs. He enacted the solidarity described in the opening section of this chapter. He opened his door, stopped giving orders, and started treating people more openly and fairly. In a sense, the CEO enacted the social resource. He realized the social partnership inside the company and the power the partnership represented in order to save it. Such intelligent leaders are not the case in all companies of the region. We have many examples of those where the leaders simply do not understand this. For instance, a company that delivers work clothing to industrial companies had the workforce go on strike after long-term disagreements with the CEO and owner. The employees wanted the same privileges that the national agreement offered, but the CEO and owner refused. The conflict gained publicity because the unions had struggled to get the companies to pay for their employees' work clothes which itself had established a huge national market for the company, although the company refused its own employees' privileges from the same agreement. The strike went on for weeks, but the CEO and owner backed down after the unions collectively made the industrial companies buy clothes from other suppliers. In other words, solidarity is a cultural resource that is reinforced by the national agreement and enacted upon effectively by skillful management. However, the resource can also be a constraint for a leader. Another example includes using wages as a form of award for doing a good job, which is limited by the national agreement. It sets the wages in accordance with function, seniority, and so on, and not performance. The local agreements should compensate for this. However, they more or less follow the same rationality of function, seniority, and so on, providing equal pay for equal work, but adjusted to the company's profit. Therefore, these agreements serve a sort of 'equalizing' force in the distribution of wealth created between the workforce and capital owners.

Leaders have, therefore, to find other ways of motivating and rewarding high-performing employees.

Another side of being a CEO is his/her role toward the customers. In an environment of changing and contradictory demands from the customers, she/he cannot be in control. Rapid decision-making in the lower organizational levels is key to the close collaboration between C6 and its customer(s). Realizing this, the new CEO changed how he led the company, and followed up with his people differently than he had initially tried. Following up projects on an overall level with 'traffic lights' on the reports as indications of the project being on track serves as an example of this. Aggregated information indicated that he trusted the project leaders and wanted to be informed, just not lead in detail.

Another feature with the changed leader role was the respect the CEO got from the organization's members. It became clear he understood the pressure and difficult working environment they all lived in. He respected the organization's identity by adding in long working hours and helping to focus the work efforts into what was important to the customer. As such, he gained respect. In many ways, he discovered that he had little or no influence over the customers and put himself in the same 'boat' as the rest of the organization. However, the CEO cannot lead the company single-handedly.

Accountant Leader's Role

In the aftermath of the financial crisis, there were discussions about the MBA programs and their value foundation (Steward, 2009). Others pointed to the behavior of the banks (Stiglitz, 2009). However, the Dahlem report focused on several reasons for the financial crisis and the systemic failure of academic economics (Colander et al., 2009). Its main point was the reliance on mathematical models that assume markets and economies are stable and rational. Winter[4] argues that the rationality assumption is wrong, claiming in an interview that people cannot be rational as they take out mortgages when they cannot afford it ('Why Economists Failed to predict the Financial Crisis,' 2009). The economists did not consider irrational behavior and believed that people act the same as individuals as in groups. Besides the behavioral aspects, there are fundamental faults in such thinking. Believing numbers and mathematical models tell the correct, complete picture of the real world without checking the validity of these premises is the major factor as to why the financial crisis was not predicted. On a micro economic level,

Johnson and Kaplan (1987) wrote about the appropriateness of the accounting system and how it fails to show important sides of the value creation. This could explain why the car manufacturers to produce more of the car models that cost them money, and fewer of those that earned them money. Cooper and Kaplan (1988a, 1988b) introduced ABC and, later, Activity-Based Management (Armstrong, 2002) to overcome these inefficiencies. The basis is to define an activity as a *'routine act performed "for" the cost-object'* (Armstrong, 2002, p. 117). All activities have associated costs which trigger more costs. A dynamic picture of variable costs relies on close attention to activities and their associated costs. Thereby, ABC is a method to overcome inefficiencies of a normal accounting system, although it still heavily relies on numbers to simplify the picture, that is, *'management by the numbers'* (ibid.).

An illustrative example involves one of the researcher's new experiences as a CFO in a large chain of sport shops. He had every shop manager attend monthly meetings, and before one of those, he received a large energy bill. During the meeting, after going through the numbers and statements, he urged the managers to start saving energy. Two weeks later, he discovered a sudden drop in sales at one of the shops. It had a prime location and there were not any indications why this drop in sales should suddenly occur. He decided to investigate this himself; it was only half an hour drive from the office. Arriving at the location the shop was dark and looked closed. The manager had turned off half the lighting in order to save energy. Immediately, he realized that the manager only followed orders, but he as the CFO had failed as a leader. First, he did not ask for reasons behind the bill and the reflection within the inquiry phase was omitted. Second, solutions were not discussed with the shop managers. He took it for granted that they knew how to save energy and no discussions were deemed to be needed. However, their job expertise is to sell sports equipment and provide services to customers. Cost savings are not their responsibility but the CFO's; he had filled his role in line with *management by numbers*. Third, from his office desk, the value chain was not visible. He needed to go to the actual spot where the activity is located. Only then did he gain insight into how cost occurs and the amount of the cost was therefore put into perspective. Fourth, he unconsciously identified himself as a decision-support manager for the CEO or owner, by giving out orders and relying on numbers with little to no reflection on whether the numbers reflected the value-creation process. This example leads us to ask the following question: Can this indicate a different management philosophy, where we trust numbers and figures the systems tell us and not the people working in the value-creation chain? On the other hand—and more to the point—economists see themselves as executives of CEO's decisions whereby there is an underlying issue of openness. How figures and numbers occur is not open, as the accounting system is—for most people—a closed one that produces numbers which decisions are based upon. To make good financial reports is to measure the factors surrounding the value-creation activities. Only then will these numbers and figures give solid support to the competitive advantage of the company.

This realization of not being open stands in contrast to how problems should be dealt with and are normally confronted in Norwegian companies. The solution is a result of discussion and reflections in collaboration among various functions. However, it requires an intimate understanding of the value-creation process, and many accountants may not be familiar with this as their work concentrates on statement figures, numbers, and schemas which are simplified economic models of the value-creation process that often focus on satisfying stock markets, governmental regulations, and so on. By not having openness, economists do not engage with the actual work process directly which could explain why Johnson and Kaplan (1987) never explicated why the numbers go wrong. Thus, understanding the work processes represented by the numbers and their connection to issues of openness and closeness to value-creation processes is vital. This means that instead of sitting in an office looking at numbers and figures, accountants, economists, and controllers should be much closer to the main sources of value-creation in the company. In this way, they could relate their figures more directly to the actual processes represented. Adding to this argument is the realization that accounting should be a strategic partner, besides HR, Operations, Development, and other departments, that places greater emphasis on openness in collecting numbers, changing the mentality from decision-support to be an active partner in value-creation activities.

During the crisis, the case companies asked the researcher to help them apply for public funding due to his background as a CFO. The main argument in obtaining such funding regarded technological innovations. He therefore insisted that the economists, controllers, and/or CFOs meet together with the developers when filling out funding applications. C3 held such meetings which discussed the items to put in the application. During one meeting, a controller showed the calculation schema for determining the price of a new part on a huge spreadsheet with lots of variables and numbers. The developers tend to be familiar with the summary page in the spreadsheet, but he wanted to understand how the variables connected, how the constants got their values, and what the routines were for updating it. The participants were silent and focused. Sometimes they updated the values and variables when a new part was calculated, otherwise the input stayed static. It came as something of a surprise to the developers who had assumed that such things were updated on regular basis with the data from production systems. Sorting this out with a promise to put together a workgroup to find out how to update input, the researcher asked a second question: Why is it on a spreadsheet when engineers use simulation to understand important technological issue? Simulation creates the opportunity to have deeper and broader understandings, additionally offering multiple results by changing the parameters and variables. He argued that a spreadsheet will not fill this role. It resulted in a lengthy discussion between developers and economists. While the developers agree with the researcher, the economists argued about the cost issue of introducing and building such a simulation system. Still today, a spreadsheet is used for the price calculation but with more updated inputs. After the meetings, both economists and developers came to the researcher and said that they better understood each other's argumentation when calculating prices, and in this sense the collaboration was useful. And we hope that the economists now understand the notion of openness and closeness to the actual value-creation process.

Beside the price calculation, there are differences between the two groups that are interesting to note. The facts and numbers of the developers and engineers are on full display in various systems and charts. However, listed in the stock market, C3 hides its economic numbers and figures. Whether this was an excuse or not was never investigated. What stands out is that the economists create a powerful position for themselves by hiding numbers. This position is actually not motivated by power gain, rather due to a management tradition and philosophy. Being in control of the price calculation with little or no insight from others places them firmly in control; however, this is just 'the way things are done.' Ultimately, it is the price and cost calculation that determine a product's destiny. Misusage of this calculation tool can turn decisions into what the misuser feels is favorable. Likewise, not updating figures and submitting wrong constant values can also influence decisions. By communicating central economic figures followed by internal openness as the foundation for calculation yields better decisions. When this openness is achieved, the numbers will be more related to the actual value-creation processes, resulting in better grounds for decision-making and this must be a central part of facilitative management.

In the other case company C6, the accounting and finance function consisted of very few people with two full-time employees handling all the numbers and reporting. Some contracted personnel helped when needed, but the main workload fell on the company's own employees. Looking at the workload, this department was under enormous pressure and had long working hours but they could not do anything else other than conventional accounting, and facts and numbers from activities were seldom analyzed. However, it turned out that the product managers did some of these analyses. The positive side effect of this was a cost awareness in the organization. The product management has the value chain in full view and can better relate the cost to each activity. In some sense, it supports the *management of costs*, not *management by numbers,* and when accounting and development departments work closely together, the projects seem to be successful; accounting can pinpoint where the value is created and measure it more precisely.

Facilitative Operation Management

The area where 'real value' creation occurs—operations—is now explored regarding what it means to manage this function. Starting with Toyota's crisis in the late 1980s and beginning of the 1990s, Ohno argued that *'standards should not be forced down from above, but rather set by production workers themselves'* (Ohno, 1988, p. 98). Even though the Toyota system was glorified by in the 1990s (e.g., Womack & Jones, 1996; Womack, Jones, & Roos, 1990), Toyota found it obsolete and changed the system between 1990 and 1992. The reason behind these changes was due to a dramatic labor shortage and exhausted supervisory staff (Shimizu, 1995). The logic of the Toyota Production System was to let the workers reflect with strong guidance from the supervisory staff. However, with young people reluctant to take on jobs characterized by the 3Ks (Shimizu, 1998),[5] the worker shortage placed a huge strain the supervisory staff had to fill. During the mid-1990s, the financial situation at Toyota was not satisfactory and the massive hiring of temporary workers resulted in huge fluctuations of production volume. Solving this second labor crisis, the temporary employees became permanent and management initiated massive training programs. On a technical level, product variances were reduced (Fujimoto, 1999) although the human side went through radical changes. The reason behind this was somewhat captured by Klein (1989) who argued for the loss of individual and team autonomy, as well as autonomy over methods. However, the management of production efficiency, wage system, training, and safety also changed (Shimizu, 1998) with time. In 2005, Mehri reported serious safety issues at Japanese production plants. Thus, even the celebrated Toyota system struggles with managing operations.

C6 also struggled with fluctuations in production volume. When there are sudden stops in the automated production lines, the root causes are difficult to locate as employees are responsible for many machines and in many cases, small production lines.[6] Such a setup requires a great deal of knowledge to understand and repair many different machines. Finding the root cause for a sudden stop is therefore difficult and the solution for making the production line more stable actually arose organically. The factory is divided into two main sections producing parts for front and rear suspensions. When problems occurred in the front production section, people from the rear area started to help, and vice versa. The practice worked well and soon both lines increased production flow. Over time, managers started to notice this practice, but by then it was easy to show the mutual increases in production and drop in production stops. It resulted in informal approval of the practice and increased interest from developers to look at what was going on at the shop floor. In an effort to increase the problem-solving capabilities there, the former CEO introduced 'task teams' led by developers that included many different functions and competences which could contribute in many ways. However, this did not work very well. Upon asking the operators why, they were reluctant to give honest answers. However, with persuasion they stated that they felt like underdogs in such situations. Developers were well-spoken and talked about how easy it was to fix this and that, and in a couple days the problem reoccurred. Now, the same people came up with another explanation without checking why the first solution did not work. It resulted in not reporting small stops and continuing the former practice of giving each other advice and help on the shop floor. The factory manager clearly knew about the practice but did not tell the CEO: '*It works better this way.*' Having people figuring out their own problems leads to motivation and learning. Underlying this statement is the fact that outsiders cannot find good solutions in an ever-changing, continuous process; they have difficulties of keeping their knowledge and insight up-to-date. In addition, the task forces, although meant to be the helping hand to operations, stand out as a key failure of Tayloristic organizations. The learning, successfully produced by mutual helping and reflection, turned into model O-I learning where the task team learned and diffused learning to operations as the problem's solution.

C6 has a production plant in Canada which is configured much the same as that of Raufoss, and the company often compared the two plants. At the beginning of the research project, the former CEO wanted the research team to investigate why maintenance took longer at Raufoss than in Canada. The easy answer was that in Canada there was more structure and preparation before scheduled maintenance by the maintenance team. In this way, every possible tool and part needed was present and no time was lost finding tools or parts.[7] However, many operators and maintenance people also pointed to the fact that Canada did not have task teams making changes all the time. The CEO thought Norwegians were reluctant to follow orders, and the Canadians just followed orders without asking questions. The research team never fully investigated this due to the financial crisis and change of CEO. Nevertheless, it seems likely that the frustration over the task teams played a part. The important thing here is to have managers who listen. In the example of the task teams, the CEO first listened and accepted the practice. Nevertheless, he later came up with his own idea, and took strong ownership regarding the task force without checking if it really helped the problem-solving process on the shop floor. Interestingly, the CEO did not insist on establishing task forces in Canada.

OEM AND SUPPLIER RELATIONSHIP

This chapter has dealt with customers as demanding and often changing their minds; however, not all customers or OEMs are following this path. The relationship between C3 and BMW illustrates an example of a collaborative relationship. C3 had delivered bumpers and crash boxes to BMW for a long time and to many different car models. This lengthy collaboration has brought the two companies closer in the lower organizational levels whereby lower and mid-management seemed to have developed mutual trust. During several interviews and working with the quality team at C3, this became obvious. The quality inspector at BMW in charge of checking C3 has said quite openly that he does not spend much time checking C3. Asking the developers at C3 in charge of products to BMW, they explained this trust as an institutional, built on serving the needs of BMW over the years. In short, C3 has shown that it knows what it is doing. This does not mean that BMW did not check C3, but it did not check so intensively and extensively as compared with its other suppliers. Technological know-how and quick response times on important requests are mentioned as other underlying explanations, with noticeably more slack and an informal development environment within the ongoing projects.

C3 worked with other important customers such as Audi/VW, Volvo/Ford,[8] GM, and Daimler by having resident engineers at the customers' site. These resident engineers secure closeness to the customers' development departments, serving as both early warning system and consulting service. This also helps to build trust on technological know-how bases. In many ways, the engineers prove that they know engineering details in depth and that the development of a part for a new car is in the best hands. C6 has discussed such a system of resident engineers, but has decided on product managers located at Raufoss. These product managers have responsibility for a product from the start of a development project, its serial production, and its end of life. This approach secures a continuum and one contact point for one car platform. It also puts the product characteristics and quality up front internally by having one responsible person. To compensate for its lack of onsite engineers, C6 sales and marketing manager travelled a lot, accompanied by product managers. The research team wondered why they travelled together and got this simple answer:

> Lots of important decisions are made very early in the discussions about a possible new development project ... therefore deep engineering insight is needed to avoid potential and additional huge investments after starting the project in order to keep the promises made to the OEM.

He agreed that it would be easier to be located closer to the customers. However, C6 did not have the economic resources to have onsite, resident engineers as this requires economic muscle and a management system that can follow up and support these 'lone' engineers. It also requires a lot from the onsite/resident engineer besides the engineering skills. Namely, his/her ability to collaborate, connect with people, know who to connect with, and so on, were noted as factors by the sales and marketing director at C3, the leader responsible for the onsite engineers. More interestingly, he also talked about his own leadership skills and education.

The Norwegian University of Science and Technology (NTNU) hands out a special ring to every master's student who completes his/her degree. This manager was proud of this ring and eager to talk about his education. Both of us in the research team who interviewed him had also studied at the university. Therefore, it was easy to talk about teachers and subjects, and relate to one another. However, the interesting part was that he claimed that in his engineering studies, he did not receive any leadership competence, even if the university claimed so at that time. When we asked him to elaborate on this statement, he said that leading the onsite/resident engineer requires a different leadership role than the management books suggest. Specifically, he argued that talking to employees on a daily basis was important, and being more of a 'father' figure than a leader when handing out orders was important. This notion of a 'father' figure is not facilitative management, but simply how this leader understood his role: '*You have to remember that these [resident] engineers are quite lonely and have to make decision many times without confronting his leader or others in his organization.*' Having people work independently puts a lot of pressure on the individual. In addition, she/he needs to know the production processes in great detail to guide the customer development teams in a favorable direction for the organization to win the contract. Specifically, '*[s/h]e [the engineer] has to know what our production processes can and cannot do, and estimate the additional cost of going outside the current capabilities of the production processes.*' This also relates to a different skill, as one resident engineer said, '*[w]orking like I do is like waking up to an exam every day.*' This means he is challenged by the OEM's development teams to discuss solutions that are also outside the product range of his own organization. In many ways, this kind of relationship is extremely close and demanding.

The collaborative relationship with BMW has not been without incidents. Isaksen and Kalsaas (2009) reported not only on trust at an engineering level but also on a lost contract after much development work. In this story, BMW wanted to go for steel instead of aluminum for cost reasons. Moreover, Isaksen and Kalsaas talked about shock waves at C3. What these researchers failed to realize is that this kind of dual development is not unusual. Projects, where part costs are critical or uncertain due to, for example, raw material prices, can be uncertain environments. From an economic perspective, it is about safeguarding or a form of hostage-taking. However, what shocked C3 was that BMW did it, not that it was done. Economic factors play an important part in developing projects, and decisions may be solely based on economic figures. In addition, in the eyes of the engineers, these decisions are often bad because they are perceived as one-sided and simplified.

The CEO and the sales and marketing director at C3 gave more detail into the background behind the BMW incident. However, the manager that initiated this is no longer working at BMW. More interestingly, these practices occur, and sometimes OEM's show technical drawings from their suppliers to competing suppliers where '*[t]he rationality ... is to get the lowest price*' (CEO and sales and marketing director). They could not think of any reason for it other than price motives on a contractual level, referring back to Williamson's (1985) hostage model. However, such behavior takes time and it is difficult for the engineers to work together after such incidents, noting that '*[i]t is very short sighted and typical [of] economists.*' One cannot collaborate on developing the best parts at low prices if there is no trust between the parties or organizations. Trust is then regarded as the opposite of opportunism as Williamson defined it (Williamson, 1979, 1996). However, it is important to understand trust and opportunism on an institutional level and how this influences trust on lower levels. Trust at a personal engineering level can quickly vanish with the discovery of hidden dual development projects. A behavior that has the sole purpose to satisfy the wallets of the owners of the big OEM can be seen as predictable in the minds of the economists who are taught transaction cost economic theory at a contractual and institutional level. However, for the engineers who are focusing on the part's development, and the effective and efficient ways to produce it, the focus is on individual or group levels.

Looking at C6, the collaborative relationship with Volvo was at the starting point. C6 had never worked with the North-European car manufacturer before, but one project member at the car manufacturer had collaborated with C6 when he worked for another North European car manufacturer. Still, there were no personal or social relationships. As mentioned in Chap. 5, the research team was surprised by how seemingly superficial one of the project audits went. However, there had been one audit before this. It went very well and there were almost no issues. The project manager at C6 also came through as a trustworthy, knowledgeable person. We believe that the second audit that the research team attended reaped the benefits from the first. And throughout the duration of the followed project this trusted relationship continued. One example that enforced the trust further was that the project leader became aware of a potential issue regarding the new solution of the ball joint on the suspension part. As we had just taught the project group the A3 method of problem-solving, he prepared an A3 report on the potential problem for representatives from the customer who thought it was very interesting and to the point. They also commented that it was easy to understand and trustworthy where the engineering become the linchpin of the project. Gradually, the research team experienced that less time was spent on checking and asking project details in the quality reports, and it seemed to speed up project work. If this is true, then trust has an economic value. Time saved on reporting was used on better solutions and turned the engineering discussions to other more important issues.

The building blocks of trust between the OEM and suppliers are important to investigate. As mentioned, historically C6 did not have success with Japanese companies. We were told that it had to do with the long-term building of trust that the Japanese required, and that profit margins did not allow for this. However, a second explanation follows the track of the BMW story, illustrated in an effort to obtain Mazda as a new customer. A few months after the initial contact and building interest at Mazda, it sent a delegation to C6. During their stay, the Mazda employees were allowed to see and ask about everything. Afterward while talking to C6's participants, they discussed on some interesting topics, and the informed, highly educated people from Mazda asked questions such that it could only be answered by exposing secrets about the production at C6: *'It was as if they wanted to know so much that they could explain to us what was wrong if they got a bad part from us.'* This reflects back to transaction cost economics and the general belief that the calculation of economic benefits is adversarial to trust. We do not know if Mazda was trying to get technological secrets from C6, but this participant's remarks made us reflect upon it.

Ultimately, the main point for facilitative management is to build the relationship in a way that economic benefits and trust are not at odds, while guiding the project or organizational members' priorities by looking at the overall business objectives. It means not spending much time on less important customers.

GENERAL ASPECTS OF FACILITATIVE MANAGEMENT

This chapter started with a discussion of the macro foundation of Norwegian work-life. The social security network built over years is an important component of feeling secure. It also described the labor cost situation in Norway and how companies had to answer to this. More importantly, the section dealt with the building of social partnerships that motivate and inform citizens on a general basis. Partnerships tend to spur volunteerism in society, and leading a company in an intelligent way can tap into this volunteerism for the firm's benefit. Thereafter, individualism and vulnerability due to different measurement systems were discussed which led specifically to the industry setting, laying the foundation for project leaders' authority through stories. How a new leader filled his role was illustrated through deep technological skills providing insight into what activities needed to be done, focusing on participant motivation and problem-solving in small groups, as well as trusting one's own abilities. This story about the new CEO demonstrated how to adapt and change his leader style to fit the needs of the organization and gain respect.

Yet another important leading position to consider is the accountant or CFO. This position deals with numbers and mathematical models of the value-creation process or '*management by numbers*.' However, this requires insight into how the value-creation process works, and must be constantly updated. Decisions often have economic models as their main support; however, wrong figures and values can lead to bad decisions. In addition, the accuracy of the results depends on the process of updating figures and values in an open environment with discussions and reflection between different functions in the organization. Alternatively, allowing the people closest to the actual activity to make the calculations and generate values can change the *management by numbers* to management by cost.

Facilitating operational management means letting people have some degree of autonomous space for problem-solving. The use of different working tools such as SMED works best when people use them in a trial-and-error fashion as this stimulates an O-II learning process. Having outsiders, no matter how 'friendly' they are, contributing to problem-solving is difficult in practice. Problem-solving in operation is a continuous process. Therefore, outsiders coming and going cannot fully tap into this. However, facilitating the process in a manner that secures continuity is just as important. This facilitative thought also concerns the OEM–supplier relationship. Close collaboration between companies will benefit both.

The section mentions two different models for close collaboration—resident engineers and travelling—that require different skills. Leading resident engineers involves understanding the loneliness and pressure faced on a daily basis, with continual updates on new abilities and changes in domestic operations. The travelling model is the more traditional sale. However, deep insight into possibilities of the operation and how the value-creation process works are just as important as in the resident model. Many important decisions are made very early in discussion of development projects with the customer and wrong information here can consequently lead to wrong decisions which could generate huge additional investments at later stages.

Generally, facilitative management is about the realization of social partnership; that is, being able to assist the problem-solving and reflection processes in order to find the best solutions, realizing that leaders do not always have the best information and insight. It regards having confidence in the people working for you which means time and space to discuss and reflect. In addition, employees need the security to suggest sometimes radical solutions, and be able to criticize the current value-creation process. Clever and intelligent leaders are also able to tap into macro foundations for work-life in general such as from the notion of 'dugnad,' and use this for the company's benefit which transfers to the employees. It is important for leaders to understand that the value-creation process, whether in offices or at the shop floor, is not necessarily visible through figures, statements, systems, and so on. These tools are simplifications of the ever-changing development process, and securing relevant updating processes becomes essential for leadership and decision-making.

Notwithstanding, for facilitative management to work, all leaders must behave according to these principles. Having one who does not follow can destroy the organizational trust needed to have effective collaborative problem-solving and reflection processes. Or, as the Spanish 'El Cid poem' says about a famous warrior: '*What a good vassal, if he only had a good lord!*' Some leaders tend to serve the stockholders, and more or less forget to serve the people working in the organization that create the values daily. The collapse of many financial companies during the crisis stands as the prime example of this behavior. However, it is easy to be led in such a direction by putting too much trust in various systems but physicalized management cannot work alone; decision systems show simplified pictures of the complex value creation in the organization. Accounting systems, as an example, usefully show trends and give the overall corporate impression, but the truly interesting part is the story behind the numbers which can make a difference in changing the organization's direction. The moral is that a clear focus on the daily value-creation system and the people making it work will also serve the stockholders in the end. By making the employees 'shine,' the leader fulfills his role, gains trust, and has a strong authority base. Leading is not about control, but more about facilitation for the organization to find good solutions to problems.

FINAL REFLECTION

Partnership or orchestration and the difficult blend of pivoting between the workforce and external stakeholders are key focal points to consider. Until now, this chapter has analyzed how different leaders behave or at least should behave, and how they manage their relationships. Beyond managing is the question of how managers understand the strategic partnership between engineers, accountants, HR staff, operators, and other members as a form of social orchestration and strategic partnership with the common goal of making profit.

Looking at the two case companies, the CEOs are engineers and often come from the same university—NTNU—as engineering graduates. Engineering problems and issues are therefore well understood. Even the HR people are often NTNU engineering graduates. Therefore, it is safe to claim that technological development and problem-solving dominate these companies. Nearly all of the NTNU engineering graduates proudly wear the university ring as a symbol of having 'the right education' and 'understanding important business things.'

However, looking at successes from the case companies, they seem to have one thing in common: getting the strategic partnership right or conducting the orchestration well. The project that gave birth to C6 was the development of suspension part for GM, the Epsilon I platform. Here, engineers and economists sat together and developed figures, budgets, measuring points, and so on. It was a huge collaborative effort. The other case company, C3, needed to improve operations dramatically in order to stay in business. Instead of putting an engineer to lead such a critical continuous improvement program, they put a theologian, an economist, and an engineer in a team, with the theologian as the leader. This program was a formidable success, winning the Toyota Supplier Award for quality and cost management for two consecutive years (2003 and 2004). One of the success stories from this period was implementing

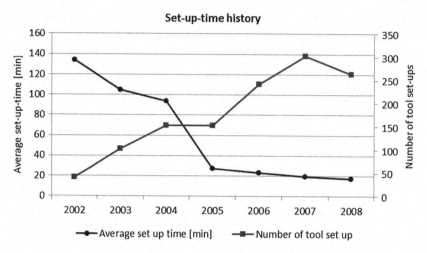

Fig. 6.1   Setup-time history (Ringen, 2010, p. 196)

the SMED tool.[9] When it was first initiated, the changeover time (stop in production) was 138 minutes. After endless changes of routines, problem-solving, and reflection meetings with all participants, this was reduced to under 20, with an increase of number of tool setups from 20 to 260 in the same period (Fig. 6.1). These results could only be achieved by a leading team with broad experience working closely together with the operators over years, exemplifying a truly collaborative effort in partnership orchestration.

Second, the focus is changed to the pivoting problem. In a hierarchal organization, one finds many people caught in the middle levels. This is especially complicated in a stock corporation due to the absentee stockowners that demand return on investments and also have the authority; the CEO is not fully autonomous. She/he therefore becomes the servant not only of the demanding customers and his/her staff, but also to the board of directors and stockholders. In the case companies, C3 is part of a stock market company and C6 is part of an international family-owned firm. Both of them have interlocking directories where people serve in many director boards (Bowman, 1996; Scott, 1997), often originating from, or appointed by, the mother company. This brings our thoughts back to the indirect rule of the British Empire (Gluckman, Mitchell, & Barnes, 1963), whereby one locally appointed chief was the regional representative put in a very difficult position at the interface of colonial and local traditions. For example, giving the chief orders that were completely incompatible with the local culture was common. Yet, if the locals did not do what the British chief had been ordered to make them do, the chief became responsible. This may also be referred to as 'intercalary' (Gluckman et al., 1963) which infers that the roles point in both directions; thus, it becomes a question of how to exist in the middle. Many leaders in modern companies are familiar with this, especially in hierarchical organizations. Hence, leaders cannot only look down into the organization, but have just as much to look up from it. Almost every manager has somebody to report to in one way or another. The idea of looking up puts boundaries around this notion of facilitative management. For instance, if the stockholders demand 5 percent return on their investment as a non-discussible demand, then the CEO may be in a difficult situation for facilitative management if the stockholders do not care how you treat the employees as long as the goal is reached.

Overall, this leads us to question whether facilitative management is something that only Norwegians can use, or an international phenomenon. No doubt that being a facilitative manager in Norway is made easier by the labor agreements, labor unions, and employer social partner discussions that provide some parameters that prevent the single focus on profit. Further, single-minded profit focus from stockholders is more common in countries such as China and Korea which would provide poor conditions for facilitative management. The OEM–supplier relationship is also something that provides poor conditions, because the OEM does not care about the supplier's employees. Even though the Norwegian model comes with social agreements, the case companies still operate in this poor OEM—supplier relationship. Still, facilitative management works successfully in companies competing on a global market. In other words, the case companies relate to markets that are outside the social partnership of Norway and appear successful. Therefore, managers have more room for conducting facilitative management than they perhaps think or wish to acknowledge. Finally, it is worth highlighting that the case companies now have much more orders from the Japanese OEM than when we—as researchers—were involved in the study which could perhaps be due to increased understandings of one another's work. To summarize, in order to be a facilitative manager you have to show certain skills such as risk taking, confidence, interpersonal skills, and demonstrating commitment to the work itself. The last feature relates to peoples' respect stemming from punctuality, working hard, and listening intently.

NOTES

1. By highly automated production lines mean huge investments in production equipment, robot, and so on that eliminate labor-intensive work. These production lines operate at high production rate and high cycle time.
2. Look at former chapter of organizational learning for more detail.
3. 'Obeya rooms' is taken from Japanese and means simply big room. Here, the project meets with many different forms, pictures, and diagrams hanging to give instant, up-to-date information about the project. For more information about how this works see Morgan and Liker (2006).
4. He is a regarded professor from Wharton in University of Pennsylvania. And he is the co-author of the famous book 'The Nature of the Firm' explaining the theories of the Nobel Prize winner R.H. Coase. The other co-author was Williamson, another Nobel Prize winner.
5. 3K's = Kitanai or dirty, Kitsui or difficult, Kiken or dangerous.
6. In many places, the production lines are divided into many small sub-lines. A small stop in one sub-line does not stop the entire production line, thereby making it more robust. It is also easier for employees because there are fewer machines to deal with, maintain, and learn about. However, each employee must still learn several machines in order to do his/her job.
7. In the Lean tradition it is called SMED (Single-Minute Exchange of Die). Principally, the dividing tool changes into external and internal. The external is about doing everything that can be done before stopping the production lines (finding hand tools, pre-warming the die, informing people, etc.) and the internal is the actual changing of die including the stop of a production line.
8. Volvo still owned by Ford at the time of interview.
9. SMED = Single-Minute Exchange of Dies production tool which means changes be made in less time by separating the internal and external setup operations. External is everything that can be done without stopping the production. The clue is to do most of the work externally so that the internal job becomes as little as possible and the production stop is kept to a minimum.

REFERENCES

Armstrong, P. (2002). The costs of activity-based management. *Accounting, Organizations and Society, 27*(1–2), 99–120. https://doi.org/10.1016/S0361-3682(99)00031-8

Bowman, S. R. (1996). *The modern corporation and American political thought: Law, power, and ideology.* University Park, PA: Pennsylvania State University Press.

Colander, D., Goldberg, M., Haas, A., Juselius, K., Kirman, A., Lux, T., et al. (2009). The financial crisis and the systemic failure of the economics profession. *Critical Review, 21*(2–3), 249–267. https://doi.org/10.1080/08913810902934109

Cooper, R., & Kaplan, R. S. (1988a). How cost accounting distorts product cost. *Management Accounting, 69*(10), 20–27.

Cooper, R., & Kaplan, R. S. (1988b). Measure cost right: Making the right decisions. *Harvard Business Review, 65*(5), 96–103.

Foss, N., Pedersen, T., Pyndt, J., & Schultz, M. (2012). *Innovating organization and management.* New York: Cambridge University Press.

Fujimoto, T. (1999). Capability building and over-adaptation: A case of 'fat design' in the Japanese auto industry. In Y. Lung, J.-J. Chanaron, & D. Raff (Eds.), *Coping with variety: Flexible productive systems for product variety in the auto industry* (pp. 261–286). Hampshire: Ashgate Publishing Limited.

Ghoshal, S., & Bartlett, C. A. (1997). *The individualized corporation: A fundamentally new approach to management: Great companies are defined by purpose, process, and people.* New York: Harper Business.

Gluckman, M., Mitchell, J. C., & Barnes, J. A. (1963). The village headman in British Central Africa. In M. Gluckman (Ed.), *Order and rebellion in tribal Africa.* London: Cohen & West.

Greenwood, D. J., & González Santos, J. L. (1992). *Industrial democracy as process: Participatory action research in the Fagor cooperative group of Mondragón.* Assen: Van Gorcum.

Hirschhorn, L. (1997). *Reworking authority: Leading and following in the postmodern organization.* Cambridge, MA: MIT Press.

Ingvaldsen, J. A., Holtskog, H., & Ringen, G. (2013). Unlocking work standards through systematic work observation: Implications for team supervision. *Team Performance Management, 19*(5/6), 279–291.

Isaksen, A., & Kalsaas, B. T. (2009). Suppliers and strategies for upgrading in global production networks. The case of a supplier to the global automotive industry in a high-cost location. European Planning Studies, Special Edition.

Johnson, H. T., & Kaplan, R. S. (1987). *Relevance lost: The rise and fall of management accounting.* Boston, MA: Harvard Business School Press.

Klein, J. A. (1989, March–April). The human cost of manufacturing reform. *Harvard Business Review,* 60–66.

Lukes, S. (2005). *Power: A radical view.* Basingstoke: Palgrave Macmillan.

Morgan, J., & Liker, J. K. (2006). *The Toyota product development system, integrating people, process and technology.* New York: Productivity Press.

Ohno, T. (1988). *Toyota production system: Beyond large-scale production.* New York: Productivity Press.

Ringen, G. (2010). *Organizational learning and knowledge in the Norwegian automotive supplier industry.* Doctor philosophiae, NTNU, Trondheim.

Scott, J. (1997). *Corporate business and capitalist classes.* Oxford: Oxford University Press.

Shimizu, K. (1995). Humanization of the production system and work at Toyota Motor Co and Toyota Motor Kyushu. In Å. Sandberg (Ed.), *Enriching production – Perspectives on Volvo's Uddevalla plant as an alternative to Lean production* (pp. 383–404). Aldershot: Ashgate Publishing.

Shimizu, K. (1998). A new Toyotaism. In M. Freyssenet, A. Mair, K. Shimizu, & G. Volpato (Eds.), *One best way?* (pp. 63–90). Oxford: Oxford University Press.

Shimokawa, K., & Fujimoto, T. (2010). *The birth of Lean.* Cambridge, MA: Lean Enterprise Institute.

Steward, M. (2009). RIP, MBA. *CNBC.com.* Retrieved from http://www.cnbc.com/id/29895258

Stiglitz, J. E. (2009). The anatomy of a murder: Who killed America's economy? *Critical Review, 21*(2–3), 329–339. https://doi.org/10.1080/08913810902934133

Why Economists Failed to Predict the Financial Crisis. (2009). Knowledge at Wharton.

Williamson, O. (1979). Transaction-cost economics: The governance of contractual relations. *Journal of Law & Economics, 22*(2), 233–261.

Williamson, O. (1985). *The economic institutions of capitalism.* New York: The Free Press.

Williamson, O. (1996). *The mechanisms of governance.* New York: Oxford University Press.

Womack, J. P., & Jones, D. T. (1996). *Lean thinking: Banish waste and create wealth in your corporation.* New York: Free Press.

Womack, J. P., Jones, D. T., & Roos, D. (1990). *The machine that changed the world: Based on the Massachusetts Institute of Technology 5-million dollar 5-year study on the future of the automobile.* New York: Rawson Associates.

CHAPTER 7

Policy Implications of the Reindustrialization of Advanced Economies

Abstract This chapter reflects upon the body of accumulated knowledge gathered in the previous chapters by identifying the key skills and sensitivities that good management teams within modern manufacturing companies should possess. Given the complexities and variability of modern manufacturing production lines and markets, the management teams must ensure they act in a facilitative manner, that is, to be able to intelligently tap into and act upon cultural understanding to unleash the creative forces and eagerness of learning embedded in the organization. Are these insights adequately embedded in modern industrial policies?

INTRODUCTION

The prospect of reindustrialization in advanced economies, no matter how enticing it sounds, presents significant challenges and dilemmas to national and regional governments. First, what are the adequate policy instruments to facilitate economic restructuring in favor of the manufacturing industry? Second, what are the implications of such a structural change for resource pools and competences in a country? Third, how will this change affect national education and research systems, as well as what types of technology and innovation policies are best suited to facilitate a transition of this kind? One of the main conclusions from previous chapters was that the

© The Author(s) 2018   135
H. Holtskog et al., *Learning Factories*, Palgrave Studies in
Democracy, Innovation, and Entrepreneurship for Growth,
https://doi.org/10.1007/978-3-319-41887-2_7

efficiency of interactions between worker, machine, and management is becoming—and perhaps it always has been—an important factor for competitive advantage in the manufacturing sector. However, is this a topic of discussion in the national reindustrialization policy agendas?

In this chapter, we review three broad policy agendas in order to identify how modern policy thinking conceives the issue of reindustrialization and what type of threats and opportunities are perceived as important in this context. A first observation to make is that a number of advanced economies increasingly recognize the fact that industry is an important component of knowledge- and value-creation in a country. Outsourcing manufacturing activities to low-cost countries, China in particular, has been a source of economic growth in the global economy and a response to emerging global production networks and interlinked markets. The long-term effects of this outsourcing wave on national knowledge bases, and perhaps on the democracies of the outsourcing economies, are however not yet fully grasped. The dominant economic doctrine posits that low-cost country manufacturing companies ought to outperform manufacturing activities in the Western world, resulting in the establishment of production sites there and maintaining the high-end activities, such as R&D and managerial functions, domestically in the West. Recent and ongoing technological advances in automation such as robotics, artificial intelligence (AI), additive manufacturing, big data analytics, and new nano- and micro materials—among others—have resulted in two mutually reinforcing effects. The first is that the share of capital to labor costs has steadily increased, rendering the importance of having access to large pools of cheap labor as the main source of competitive advantage. The other is that the increasingly complex interactions between a small number of workers and advanced equipment in the factory floors favor flexible high-skilled/high-salary workers and technicians. These two effects render the participative and democratic modes of work organization a significant source of competitive advantage if properly managed. Specifically, in this policy overview, we focus on the OECD's project 'the next production revolution,' the EU's Manufuture initiative on Germany's strategy Industry 4.0, and the Swedish policy initiative.

OECD

The OECD points to the significant productivity gains and the many unexploited opportunities detected in the interface of a multitude of new production technologies, but also to serious concerns in many countries over the loss of work to machines. Historically, there has been overwhelming evidence that beyond job losses, the total effect of technological change on output prices, wages, and profits, as well as on job creation resulting from the continuous restructuring of the economy due to technological change, has been positive. Having said that, the adverse effects of technological progress on, for example, the environment do not seem to have been thoroughly considered in the OECD's reckoning.

MANUFUTURE: AN EUROPEAN UNION INITIATIVE

Manufuture was launched in 2004 in the Netherlands with the publication of 'Manufuture—a Vision for 2020.' High-ranking representatives from European industry and the scientific community commissioned the project. Its vision for the manufacturing industry's development has been central for several EU research framework programs, initially pointing toward some key societal drivers:

- Completion, especially from emerging economies
- The shortened lifecycle of enabling technologies
- Environmental and sustainability issues
- Socio-economic environment
- Regulatory climate
- Values and public acceptance

These key drivers could be met by investment in five priority pillars:

- New high-added-value products and services
- New business models
- New manufacturing engineering
- Emerging manufacturing science and technologies
- Transformation of existing RTD and educational infrastructures to support world-class manufacturing, fostering researcher mobility, multidisciplinary, and lifelong learning

Further, megatrends that have an impact on manufacturing are built on the key drivers or challenges. These trends are as follows:

- Ageing—impact on future markets and products, human work, and organization
- Individualism—customized products, human relations, and working conditions

- Knowledge in global ICTs—knowledge driven product development, optimization of manufacturing processes, Internet Protocols, and IT security
- Globalization—process-standards in OEMs, product and manufacturing technologies for the global markets, local conditions and regulations, and location competition
- Urbanization—environment, mobility, traffic, new products for megacities, work in megacities, and factories in urban environments
- Sustainability—priorities for economic, ecologic, and social efficiency of manufacturing

To meet these listed drivers and challenges, Europe—or the EU—has developed a strategy for the future factory as '[m]anufacturing is a key enabler for Europe's grand societal challenges' (EFFRA, 2013a). A key player is the European Factories of the Future Research Association (EFFRA) that has a vision stating that 'innovative sustainable manufacturing is the key enabler and driver for the success and competitiveness of all European industries' (ibid., p. 13). The main outline of this strategy is presented in Fig. 7.1.

The figure shows that major challenges and opportunities give input into research and innovation priorities in the same way that technologies and

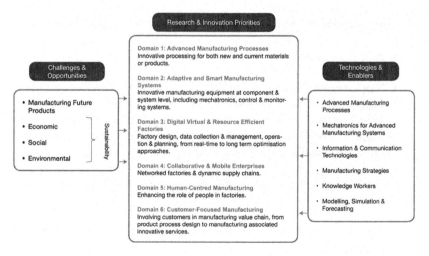

Fig. 7.1 Factories of the Future roadmap framework (EFFRA, 2013b)

enablers do. These challenges, opportunities, technologies, and enablers are syntheses of the key drivers and megatrends, aiming for the creation of socially sustainable, safe, and attractive workplaces. The development of new technologies creates knowledge-intensive workplaces and keeps manufacturing industries in Europe competitive. The roadmap argues for the mutual development of technologies and workplaces. However, it is more concrete when it comes to technology than workplaces.

Specifically, many European countries have their own initiative for their manufacturing industry. In Germany, the initiative is called Industry 4.0 with a strong focus on cyber physical systems. In the Netherlands, it is called Network Centric Production with a focus on communication and collaboration between different actors and technology. Sustainable Production in Sweden focuses on the three dimensions for the triple bottom line. These three countries show different approaches to implementing ideas for the factory of the future.

INDUSTRY 4.0: THE GERMAN INITIATIVE

Germans talk about the fourth industrial revolution or Industry 4.0. The first revolution was driven by steam power and engines. The second revolution focused on mass production and assembly lines. Electricity played a key role as an enabling technology. The third revolution introduced robots and computers to the mass production facilities and assembly lines. Automated factories speeded up the production and needed different qualifications of the operators and ultimately, different organization and management.

Internet of Things is a central concept in the German initiative. Putting sensors and electronic tags on parts with the ability to electronic communication open up new ways of designing both the factories of the future and more sustainable value chains, leading to more flexible production and self-adjusting production lines that rapidly change setup by reading the sensors on the part that comes next in the line. The sensor carries the production information needed to change the production. In this way, parts production can just as well be produced in a chaotic way rather than in batches. And other example is putting sensors on robots that detect their surroundings. It enables robots and humans to work side-by-side without danger. In the extended value chain, from factory gate to product end of life (EOL), it is also foreseeable that product connectivity may help consumers utilize the product as intended, maintain and replace parts, receive services when needed, and deliver the product at an appropriate location for securing de-assembly and distribution of materials toward a circular economy. It is this blend of Internet of Things in the real world in a complex system that is called cyber physical systems.

There are many views on what Industry 4.0 is really about; Lee, Bagheri, and Kao (2015) introduce the 5C architecture.

- Configure—supporting supervisory control and required actions. Taking away unwanted actions.
- Cognition—support decision-making by prioritize and optimize decisions.
- Cyber—refers to the technology part of a fleet of machines communicating with each other. They are able to compare their status and adjust the work after each other.
- Conversion—is about prognostics and health management of machines and components. Sensors give input about how worn a component is.
- Connection—is the different sensors, selection of effective sensors and monitoring the connection between them.

The architectural framework helps to implement Cyber-Physical Systems for 'better product quality and system reliability with more intelligent and resilient manufacturing equipment' (Lee et al., 2015, p. 22). Findings from prognostics monitoring system illustrate this technological focus where four key impact areas emerge:

- Machine health prediction reduces the machine downtime
- The information flows make industrial management more transparent and organized
- Reduce labor costs and provide better working environment
- Reduce the cost of energy by optimizing maintenance schedule and supply chain management (Lee, Kao, & Yang, 2014)

The sensors gather lots of data and information. Analyzing big data is one other key ingredient of Industry 4.0. Information and Communication Technology (ICT) plays a central role in the whole concept. Connecting hardware and software on one side and cyber and physical on the other create new collaboration productivity (Schuh, Potente, Wesch-Potente, Weber, & Prote, 2014). Even though the official documents talk about the smarter and more flexible organization little work and focus are offered to investigate this dimension. For instance, having the data and computational power to analyze them only enables us to do things that we were not capable of before. However, having individuals, teams, and organizations that can frame and reframe problems and challenges, hypothesize effects and outputs from different input signals, and predict relativeness between set of factors is still an asset in a context of Industry 4.0. The development of AI will certainly help humans in developing advanced patterns and algorithms for further productivity increase, but the initial state of a machine and a system should be understood by those involved in order to conduct continuous improvement, feel job enrichment, evolve technology and knowledge, and see the particular machine/job in a broader context. The 'technological singularity' is a hypothetical event where AI (intelligent computers, computer networks, or robots) will be capable of recursive self-improvement, progressively redesigning itself, or autonomously building a smarter and more powerful machines than itself. The discussion of when machine outperforms humans is not new. Turing (1950) addressed this topic in 1950, during the early stages of building computational machines, proposing the 'imitation game' to distinguish a machine from a man. These visions of the future, and his introduction to AI, is still valid and actual 60 years later.

An Illustration of the Industry 4.0 Vision

A large German company delivering ICT solutions presented a vision for the Industry 4.0 by establishing test plants and selling the idea where software was regarded as vital. By highlighting four main issues—speed, flexibility, quality, and efficiency—the company aims to give its customers a great leap into the factories of the future: speed means shortening time to market; flexibility means producing different products in the same production line with various quantities; sensor introduction on robots means having them coexist alongside humans at the assembly line, increasing quality; and, overall, every piece working seamlessly together will improve efficiency, giving European industry the future competitive advantage.

These headlines are interesting and somewhat bewitching. However, when assessing the details of Industry 4.0, the concept can mean something rather different. A central part of the system is the building of a twin, cyber model of the factory. The digital twin takes advantage of all the sensors in the production and the work done in the development and design phase. Testing new products and improvements in cyber space before introducing it to the shop floor is the selling point. By doing it this way, management can validate and optimize the production line. However, we believe this is redundant as it is just a digital version of scientific management, where one part of the company learns by monitoring the rest and calculating changes. Finished, optimized changes will then be communicated through instructions to the people on the shop floor. As the idea is to have a digital twin that is the true digitalization of the reality, only highly educated people can make changes and validate them. Every continuous improvement will therefore become difficult and the commitment it needs from the people working at the shop floor will vanish. It goes against the fundamental principle of Lean and continuous improvements (Bessant, Caffyn, & Gallagher, 2001; Holtskog, 2013a, 2013b; Hutchins, 2008; Liker, 2004).

Sustainable Production: The Swedish Initiative

The Swedish initiative brings attention toward sustainable production. The vision for 2030 states 'Production in Sweden is knowledge-intensive, flexible, efficient, and environmentally sustainable, made with minimal use of resources' (Teknikföretagen, 2015, p. 4). This vision is based on global trends and the Swedish challenge to meet these (Teknikföretagen, 2015). The initiative's main items are outlined as follows:

- Sustainability and effective use of resources—remanufacturing of product is the essential element. The Swedish answer is to develop new business models with strong focuses on the difficulties of remanufacturing and recycled products or material use.
- New types of production—the use of lightweight material and the integration of mechanical and ICT-based features in the products. For this challenge, the utilization of existing production knowledge and the development of new production methods will give the Swedes an advantage.
- Raw material shortage and new exotic materials—more and more industries experience raw material shortage and an increasing number of new materials are introduced to the market. Sweden must be part of the development of new materials to ensure the efficient use of raw materials through good manufacturing processes.
- Everything communicates—a continuous exchange of information between people, machines, and systems. Data management and the knowledge needed to utilize and develop business of the new opportunities is the Swedish answer.

- A challenging demographic development—with low birthrates in both Europe and Sweden, the population is becoming increasingly older. Increasing retirement age, and making the jobs more knowledge-intensive could be a solution. However, it requires more skilled and educated people and more automated processes.
- Components with micro- and nano-structures—these components are ICT-related micro components that form the backbone of sensors. In addition, Swedish leadership in the research of graphene is central. Sweden must have a string focus on efficient and effective production of micro- and nano-structures.

So far, both Swedish and German initiatives are quite similar in their interpretation of the trends and challenges for their respective societies. What separate the two initiatives are the solutions or pathways. The German initiative is centralized on technology solutions, and the Swedes have some complementary views (Teknikföretagen, 2015, pp. 10–11):

- 'Environmentally sustainable production— minimize resource consumption and environmental impact of production system and products.
- Flexible manufacturing processes—develop manufacturing processes for the products of the future.
- Virtual production development and simulation—enable conversion of information and data into knowledge and decision support in virtual and physical production systems.
- Human-centered production system—the demographic situation and the new forms and systems of interaction and collaboration between people and advanced automation to achieve high performance.
- Product- and production-based services—the major challenge are product and production-based systems based.
- Integrated product and production development—strengthen product development processes, developing processes and tools for innovative product development. ...'

Most of solutions are dealing with technology, but the focus on sustainability seems to be stronger than the German initiative. Interestingly, the Swedes also clearly emphasize the importance of humans in the vision for the factories of the future. More rapid changes and adaptive production require/ create new skills and more adaptable team organization. Decentralized decision-making and greater responsibility at the operator level are some of the central points of the future organization. Direct collaboration and continuous improvement with robots clearly indicates a new level of education. Engineers and other knowledge workers can be the new operators or blue-collar workers. Sweden not only looks at the aging population as a problem, but also analyzes how to utilize their knowledge when younger engineers enter the shop floor and redesign production. This is in accordance to the values and traditions of the Nordic work-life system.

In the policy document by the research institute Friedrich Ebert Stiftung (Buhr, 2015), the lack of human focus in Industry 4.0 is commented upon: '*Even if the issue has so far been analysed and driven from a purely technical standpoint, people remain an integral part of a decentralized and self-organized Industry 4.0.*' As workplaces will change due to new technology implementations, the research institute argues the key areas should include paying attention to the Industry 4.0 paradigm policymakers. Essentially, more complex tasks and more dynamic value-creation networks demand high degrees of flexibility and learning (ibid.): '*Machines work well for standardized production and will be there to assist people in preparing and making better decisions. In other words, people ask better questions—and machines should help them giving better answers.*' However, there are little or no indications how this assisting machine paradigm will work beside the technical visions that already exist in Industry 4.0 descriptions.

WHAT ARE THE MANAGERIAL IMPLICATIONS OF THE VISIONS FOR FUTURE FACTORIES?

In Chap. 6, facilitative management regarded features of management and leadership. High automation and technological advancement characterized the case companies as they needed to go in this direction of high automation and advanced technology in order to stay competitive in the global industry of automotive parts. The direction is—to a certain degree—similar, but not as advanced as the predictions and vision of Industry 4.0 or European reindustrialization. Therefore, it is interesting to look at the case companies and their organization as the starting point to unveil some organizational aspects of factories of the future. It can provide insights into the new research arena. First, we highlight that the challenge of an aging population cannot only be solved by rearranging the workplace for the elderly. Making people work longer is important; however, there are other important issues with age and experience. The main question should be how companies utilize experienced workers to gain or sustain a competitive advantage.

Taking the preceding discussion into consideration, there are many questions of interest, for example: Is implementing state-of-the-art digital solutions that even younger generations do not fully comprehend the solution? What will more people with higher education levels entering the shop floor mean? How will this facilitate or require new styles of management or leadership? How do people react to the possibility that management can measure each individual's performance every waking hour? With traceability down to each individual's process, will this provide a tool for monitoring both how hard one works, but also the degree of work quality? Essentially, how would management use this powerful tool?

These are just a few practical questions in the wake of reindustrialization efforts. There are of course many more. It is more relevant in this book to ask: Can facilitative management can be a powerful tool in the factories of the future?

Team organization is common in manufacturing. This basic building block in organizations plays an essential role when it comes to continuous improvement and how to set up the various processes. In an increasingly automated production line, these teams become smaller. This reinforced tendency will continue in Industry 4.0. The role of the operator will transit from stationary- and machine-specific toward a more demand-driven and task-based position. The system will instantly tell the operator where and when to prioritize, whether it is about refilling buffers, preventive maintenance, tool change, and so on. The monitoring can be done from remote, and resources be requested based on the nature of the task. In many cases, the demand for a constant pool of manpower can be reduced considerably. To extend this reasoning, will the future operator be both so specialized, flexible, and autonomous that he/she can serve multiple factories? This scenario is likely to happen as we see such centralized pools of technologists within engineering, maintenance, consultants, and so on. Such an organization challenges how we think about teams, roles, and activities. Hence, this basic building block changes fundamentally.

Facilitative management is based on several pillars. Fundamental is social partnership whereby organizations bring people together to be part of a common destiny. Democratic values, such as representation in the board of directors, broad discussions on important issues, representative selection, and so on, are just as important in an organization as in a society. The benefits include ownership of decisions, informed employees, increased motivations for suggesting improvement, and that small disagreements will stay small, and so on. However, this democratic process takes courage to implement. In some ways, it includes trusting the processes of discussions and representatives' elections. Fast decision-making and authoritarian leadership style are then outdated. However, social partnership is a fragile construction and it takes very little to break trust which serves as its foundation. One smart tool for preserving trust is built into the Nordic model with collaborating partners when it comes to work-life issues such as wage settings and the working environment.

Reindustrialization initiatives include the use of new technologies. This means that leaders will not have the best knowledge of the various processes anymore, having to rely more on their employees for advice. In light of this, the notion of facilitative management is well-suited. Building on the realization that the employees create business value, it is therefore up to management to organize business in such a way that managers create the best possible value. Such facilitative management turns traditional thinking about leadership on its head, moving away from leading people toward facilitating and serving employees in their value-creation processes. To facilitate and serve must be based on an understanding of cultures and how people socialize. We tend to use clues to manifest groups and build informal behavioral rules. Tapping into these clues and rules can therefore be a powerful leadership tool.

Finally, the organizational structure needs to be evaluated. Hierarchal structures occupy many companies where clear communication lines and decision delegation are some of the benefits. However, social partnership will challenge this structure and the leaders will experience a pivoting problem between levels (Holtskog, Martinsen, Skogsrød, & Ringen, 2016). Democratic decision-making lower down and orders from above are difficult to exercise and balance. Basic organizational principles in use today have not changed for years and we believe that new technologies will force the owners and managers to rethink how they organize, to which facilitative management could be instrumental. Flat and informal organizations, therefore, may be a good starting point.

Conclusion

The effort of European reindustrialization must gain momentum if European countries want to preserve and develop their competitiveness. The highly discussed German initiative Industry 4.0 seems to lack a clear orientation toward people and organization. Some solutions seem too technologically centered, forgetting the increased complexity when introducing people to technological solutions. Essentially, reindustrialization must take people and organization into account as they are the significant components of the factories of the future. As such, it is vital that organizations include people as vital to their long-term planning process, an area which requires more research.

REFERENCES

Bessant, J., Caffyn, S., & Gallagher, M. (2001). An evolutionary model of continuous improvement behaviour. *Technovation, 21*(2), 67–77.

Buhr, D. (2015). *Social innovation policy for industry 4.0*. Retrieved from http://www.fes-2017plus.de

EFFRA. (2013a). *EFFRA: Introduction to our association*. Retrieved from http://www.effra.eu/index.php?option=com_content&view=article&id=122&Itemid=121

EFFRA. (2013b). *Factories of the future: Multi-annual roadmap for the contractual PPP under Horizon 2020*. Retrieved from http://www.effra.eu/index.php?option=com_content&view=category&id=85&Itemid=133

Holtskog, H. (2013a). Continuous improvement beyond the Lean understanding. *Procedia CIRP, 7*(0), 575–579. https://doi.org/10.1016/j.procir.2013.06.035

Holtskog, H. (2013b). Lean and innovative: Two discourses. In H. C. G. Johnsen & E. Pålshaugen (Eds.), *Hva er innovasjon? Perspektiver i norsk innovasjonsforskning. Bind 2: Organisasjon og medvirkning – en norsk modell?* (pp. 45–64). Oslo: Cappelen Damm Akademisk.

Holtskog, H., Martinsen, K., Skogsrød, T., & Ringen, G. (2016). The pivoting problem of Lean. *Procedia CIRP, 41*, 591–595.

Hutchins, D. C. (2008). *Hoshin Kanri: The strategic approach to continuous improvement*. Aldershot: Gower.

Lee, J., Bagheri, B., & Kao, H. (2015). A cyber-physical systems architecture for industry 4-0-based manufacturing systems. *Manufacturing Letters, 3*, 18–23.

Lee, J., Kao, H., & Yang, S. (2014). Service innovation and smart analytics for industry 4.0 and big data environment. *Procedia CIRP, 16*, 3–8.

Liker, J. (2004). *The Toyota way: 14 management principles from the world's greatest manufacturer*. New York: McGraw-Hill.

ManuFuture A Vision for 2020. (2004). Retrieved from http://www.manufuture.org/wp-content/uploads/manufuture_vision_en1.pdf

Schuh, G., Potente, T., Wesch-Potente, C., Weber, A., & Prote, J. (2014). Collaboration mechanisms to increase productivity in the context of industrie 4.0. *Procedia CIRP, 19*, 51–56.

Teknikföretagen. (2015). *Made i Sweden 2030*. Retrieved from https://www.teknikforetagen.se/globalassets/i-debatten/publikationer/produktion/made-in-sweden-2030-engelsk.pdf

Turing, A. (1950). Computing machinery and intelligence. *Mind, 59*(236), 433–460.

CHAPTER 8

Conclusion

Abstract This chapter concludes by summing up and outlining the implications of the research, as well as the contributions to theory, policy, and practice. It returns the arguments to the meso and macro levels of the economy within the manufacturing sector. We argue that insights about facilitative management are key ingredients in securing conditions for a robust and competitive manufacturing sector in advanced economies. This way, we present an optimistic view and prospects as to how the advanced economies can sustain their competitiveness in balance with fundamental principles of inclusive and facilitative to learning work environments, a cornerstone in the institutional setting of the Nordic model, but also in balance with the more general qualities of openness and tolerance in modern societies and democracies. From this perspective, it is important that modern industrial policies also embrace "soft" policies about managerial styles in modern manufacturing in addition to investments in manufacturing R&D, measures stimulating open innovation practices and funding of manufacturing test-bed infrastructures.

© The Author(s) 2018   149
H. Holtskog et al., *Learning Factories*, Palgrave Studies in
Democracy, Innovation, and Entrepreneurship for Growth,
https://doi.org/10.1007/978-3-319-41887-2_8

INTRODUCTION

This chapter started by asking the overall question: How do industries create knowledge? Two theoretical traditions were briefly mentioned: strategy and employee-driven innovations (EDI). The strategy tradition focuses on how management and organizational design form competitive advantage, while EDI point toward the close collaboration between the two organizational roles, namely management and employee. Looking into manufacturing companies, the reality seems more complex. As matrix organizations make organizational roles more diffuse, the leader becomes more of a facilitator than the person who knows best. These cues triggered some questions which were the foundations of this research:

1. How do industries create knowledge?
   (a) How can organizational learning be aided inside a matrix organization?
   (b) How will an understanding of organizational culture help the creation process?
   (c) How can management or leadership facilitate learning?

The contextual base of two Norwegian automotive manufacturing companies formed the basis of this research, although Chap. 2 discussed the effect of the financial crisis on seven companies within the industrial park of Raufoss, where the two cases are located. This context chapter set the stage for the multi-dimensional and multi-causal analysis due to nested systems, or subsystems in subsystems. Thereafter, the methodology and research strategy were discussed. Cartesian doubt formed the beginning of the discussion which had the aim to challenge existing knowledge and rethink ideas or assumptions. This was done through triangulation and developed into a multi-dimensional analysis. Action research was the initial research strategy; however, changes due to the extraordinary times forced its modification whereby insider ethnography is presented because researching complex nested systems demands additional knowledge from the researcher. In this case, with technology companies, the researcher must have some degree of technological insight for analyzing the data and drawing conclusions on a higher level. The assumptions and theoretical framework followed from this, concluding that the world is a meaning-making construction to which people may, or may not, agree on. However, people in the organization still manage to work together without such mutual agreement and understanding which support the multi-dimensional and multi-causal analysis. Put differently, the chapter investigates organizational behaviors for knowledge creation or learning with multi-causality within multi-dimensional nested systems, where three main dimensions discussed are as follows: organization learning, organization culture, and facilitative management. Learning theory deals with how learning is realized within the organization as a theory of action and that formal systems do not necessarily reflect how practice functions. Organizational culture, communication arenas, and facilitative management are more important than claimed competitive advantages such as structure. Martin's (1992) perspective of differentiated culture perspectives supports the multi-dimensional analysis this thesis offers. Inconsistency in relations and channeling ambiguity outside the subcultures are the main components in this perspective. However, Martin's perspective is amplified and deepened by Geertz's (1973) analytical tool, thick description, and sense-making. The other theoretical dimensions in the analysis—facilitative management and matrix organization—demonstrate that technology changes the organization and the employees' autonomous abilities. These changes challenge the leadership role and also how the leader thinks about power use in matrix organizations.

Looking at one specific development project in detail, the espoused theory and theory-in-use differ. Defensive actions and learning model O-I are illustrated in how the quality system tools are used—the FMEA case. However, this is not because the formal systems or espoused theory are not important. The formal systems serve an important function by focusing on what to learn, creating a common language for participants, and guiding the knowledge-creation process. However, it has been shown that even in very organized development projects, the theory-in-use differs. In addition, questions on interconnectedness and interdependent parts of a social system for developing new products are raised, indicating nested systems. From this, cultural aspects follow which are illustrated by different stories, starting with the asymmetrical relationship between supplier and OEM. Understanding how people make sense of, for example, an environment with contradictory demands, stressful workplaces, and huge workloads is essential in understanding the foundation for the learning process. Demanding relationships, 'competing against the odds,' and 'crisis create heroes' are examples these and provide an understanding of engineers, not as scientific thinkers as they themselves like to think, rather as master craftsmen with little interest in documentation. This understanding of hero stories also demonstrates dimensions of inconsistency in the culture.

Inconsistencies are first analyzed according to Martin's differentiated culture dimension and then amplified and broadened by using Geertz to bring the cultural analysis one step further. Systems of symbols in the organization establish powerful moods and motivations. The voice of the customer reinforces these factors. In addition, various ways of creating knowledge, illustrated by types of developers, broaden the picture and show how homogenous a subculture really is. Sense-making processes illustrate how people formulate conceptions, as well as create auras of factuality and realism. This process includes factors such as the local community, being at the forefront of engineering and material science, customer dialogue, and the formation of formal work systems. We believe that this broadening, deepening, and amplifying is a contribution to organizational cultural theory.

Facilitative management starts with the realization of the social partnership that forms organizations. With this in mind, the main managerial task becomes how to facilitate differentiated cultures and social partners or groups to work together and create knowledge. Collaborative work among the social partners is a formidable competitive advantage. People contribute to value creation what they know best. Chapter 6 starts with a paradox; a successful Norwegian manufacturing industry competing on a global market despite being a world-class leader in high labor costs. Other macro-foundations in Norwegian work-life are highlighted to show that an intelligent leader knows how to enact on societal factors to the company's benefit and beyond. Personal abilities of a facilitative leader discussed include technological skills, insight into central value-creation activities, motivational focus, problem-solving in small groups, and trust in one's own abilities, such as being able and willing to take calculated risks. However, the argument shows that a broad range of functions need to be included in the social partnership. Accounting is one such function that needs to be addressed as a strategic partner, not as a conventional decision-support mechanism.

In social collaboration, with time to reflect on value creation, some impressive results can be achieved (see set-up-time history in the 'final reflections' section of Chap. 8). It is essential to problem-solving and reflection processes in the social partnership that the best solutions are found. Working hard and listening intently can be somewhat mantras. However, it is important to point out the pivoting problem a leader faces, caught in the middle between 'competing' levels of bottom-up and top-down pressures. Forgetting the impressive results, shortsighted partners can do much damage. Nevertheless, we strongly believe that leaders have more room for creating facilitative space in their organizations than they perhaps think or wish to acknowledge.

This brief summary of the book's chapters is an effort to answer the research questions. The 'organizational learning' section in Chap. 5 answers Question 1a, where the conclusions point to the next two chapters regarding organizational culture and facilitative management. These cultural and management factors are important in manufacturing industries for creating a model O-II learning organization which answers Question 1b. Cultural understanding helps us to understand that there is no need for a unified organizational culture, if it is even possible at all. Insight into differentiated culture will provide guidance to how this can help solve problems and enhance value-creation activities. However, it clearly demonstrates the need for specific leadership as posed in Question 1c. Facilitative management starts with the acknowledgement of the social partnership that forms the organization. The leader's role is to tap into the knowledge possessed by different partners and make them focus on solving problems in a collaborative manner, while at the same time, fight to make room for such management style among the stakeholders—the pivoting problem.

WHY IS THIS RESEARCH IMPORTANT?

As noted, today's companies rely on technology, even in service and education sectors. However, this technology is of no use if the people in the organization cannot utilize it or do not have the knowledge to deal with it in a productive way. By saying this, we indicate that there is a continuous learning process underneath its reliance. Learning can be both individual and organizational but both of them are guided by culture in some way. Nevertheless, culture is not something concrete or holistic. To truly understand culture in an organization, the differentiated culture perspective gives some support. In addition, Geertz's notion of religion provides support for understanding internal organizational contradictions which will guide leaders in their task of facilitating the learning process for knowledge creation.

Second, formal systems are equally important. In many ways, they represent the organization's (explicit) knowledge. However, formal systems have other important tasks such as focusing the learning process for the knowledge to be used productively, boxing in the creativity, and creating a common language.

Facilitative management is essentially to tap into human knowledge and make more productive use of it. In order to do this successfully, the leader has to understand the differentiated culture and contradictions, and use formal systems intelligently to capture knowledge and guide the creation process. All this requires social and strategic partnership, as illustrated in the section on the accounting department in Chap. 6. Accounting should not be a decision support function, but rather provide good measurements for value-creating activities, thereby giving directions based on insight into these activities. Doing it this way will enforce the competitive advantages of organizations.

In the financial crisis, the Lehman Brothers and AIG went bankrupt due to poor risk management. If you put risk management into the quality management discussion in this chapter, an interesting question arises: Was risk management really based on values from a true value-creation process? If not, the leaders in these companies made terrible decisions based on data that bore no relation to reality. Such a simple question reveals a fundamental fault in management thinking. Social and strategic partnership thinking could prevent leaders from making such terrible decisions. Instead of having parts of the organization as decision support, data accumulated to support leaders' decisions should arrive as collaborative learning and knowledge creating processes close to the value-creating processes. In addition, the leaders' main task is not only to make decisions but also to facilitate collaborative learning and knowledge creation.

FURTHER RESEARCH

There are many challenges that need to be further researched in order to understand this line of thought regarding competitiveness and leadership:

First, how can the concept of facilitative management be 'exported' to other/sister companies? If one manager creates a facilitative environment, can it be implemented in different companies in different countries and cultures? This is important because many companies have factories all around the world and want to have some sort of foundation for management. To research this, we intend to use a different company with production plants around the world as a case. This case company has invited some researchers to investigate the implementation of its management system around the world. Its management system has some similarities with the facilitative management described here.

Second, how to move craftsmanship culture toward more analytical problem-solving is an issue that requires attention. Changing general thinking in these organizations about what is needed to generate knowledge or assumptions.

Third, how to gain incredible results through collaborative efforts will be the central focus in another project where a company delivering thrusters for positioning ships worldwide needs to improve its quality management efforts. It wants to create quality at the source or in the mind of the workers, not only through formal systems and certifications. Here, the collaborative effort of building and implementing quality systems will be tested, as well as how the espoused theory can be kept 'up-to-date' with the theory-in-use. The company will learn from the automotive industry.

Fourth, we believe that conducting action research with companies requires insight into various fields of knowledge at the researcher's disposal, that is, you need to 'talk' the language, have technological insight, and so on. With regard to the types of insight and requirements required for this research, we believe that being close to, or an 'insider' in, the participating companies will bring much richer and fruitful insights than traditional research visits.

FINAL REMARKS

This multi-dimensional and multi-causal research in nested systems shows the importance of such an approach to research. Learning or knowledge creation as a human endeavor is multi-dimensional whereby data or findings can have more than one meaning. In addition, our reality is nested into different agreeable 'facts' or models that sometimes form systems. Therefore, conducting social research in organizations is, by nature, multi-dimensional. The organization itself is a result of sense-making activities among its members, often with many subcultures. Adding to the complexity is the relationship the organization has with outsiders, forming subsystems upon subsystems. In this picture, the manager's greatest challenge is to manage these complex internal and external relationships without having the company fall apart.

The examples offered here illustrate a general development in modern society. Leading learning organizations are not limited to technology driven organizations. In the service sector, the 'product' is consumed when it is produced, thereby making it increasingly difficult to lead the 'production' and 'development.' We believe that in the traditional service sector, facilitative management is especially important. Facilitating employee training to provide good service and helping in difficult situations are tasks that demand strong cultural understandings. How the facilitation and partnership together form competitive advantage in trade will be powerful topics to investigate.

The health sector brings in yet another dimension that further complicates this thinking. Here, there are no 'products' as such. The service result is measured on the well-being of humans which could be extremely applicable to facilitative management. Moreover, the education sector illustrates another interesting aspect of facilitative management. Often the leader does not have the greatest insight and/or is not the best educated, and strong personalities and professional beliefs stand in contrast to each other. This creates the potential to rip the organization apart with conflict. Providing social partnership and facilitating collaborative efforts will be a formidable challenge for any leader in this sector.

Overall, there are similar leader challenges in many sectors. Tapping into the belief of facilitation and partnership, management theory can change, and the theory of competitive advantage will have another important and powerful dimension. Moving leadership and decision-making closer to the 'true' value-creation processes reveals hidden capabilities. Harvesting these intelligently through the strong belief in human ability can create value for all stakeholders, not only those who hold shares.

REFERENCES

Geertz, C. (1973). *The interpretation of cultures.* New York: Basic Books.
Martin, J. (1992). *Cultures in organizations: Three perspectives.* New York: Oxford University Press.

References

Andersen, B. (1999). *Business process improvement toolbox.* Milwaukee: ASQ Quality Press.

Argyres, N., Felin, T., Foss, N., & Zenger, T. (2012). Organizational economics of capability and heterogeneity. *Organization Science, 23*(5), 1213–1226.

Argyris, C., & Schön, D. (1996). *Organizational learning II: Theory, method, and practice.* Reading: Addison-Wesley Publishing Company.

Armstrong, P. (2002). The costs of activity-based management. *Accounting, Organizations and Society, 27*(1–2), 99–120. https://doi.org/10.1016/S0361-3682(99)00031-8

Arrow, K. (1969). *The organization of economic activity: Issues pertinent to the choice of market versus nonmarket allocation.* Paper presented at the analysis and evaluation of public expenditure, PPB System, Washington.

Bessant, J., Caffyn, S., & Gallagher, M. (2001). An evolutionary model of continuous improvement behaviour. *Technovation, 21*(2), 67–77.

Bowman, S. R. (1996). *The modern corporation and American political thought: Law, power, and ideology.* University Park, PA: Pennsylvania State University Press.

Braczyk, H.-J., Cook, A., & Heidenreich, M. (Eds.). (2004). *Regional innovation system: The role of governances in a globalized world.* London: Routledge.

Brennan, L. (2001). Total quality management in a research and development environment. *Integrated Manufacturing Systems, 12*(2), 94–102.

Bruner, E. M., & Plattner, S. (1984). *Text, play, and story: The construction and reconstruction of self and society: 1983 Proceedings of the American Ethnological Society.* Prospect Heights, IL: Waweland Press.

© The Author(s) 2018   157
H. Holtskog et al., *Learning Factories*, Palgrave Studies in
Democracy, Innovation, and Entrepreneurship for Growth,
https://doi.org/10.1007/978-3-319-41887-2

Buhr, D. (2015). *Social innovation policy for industry 4.0.* Retrieved from http://www.fes-2017plus.de

Caniëls, M. (1999). *Regional growth differentials.* PhD, Maastricht University.

Clarkson, K. W., Miller, R. L., & Muris, T. J. (1978). Liquidated damages v. penalties. *Wisconsin Law Review, 54,* 351–390.

Coase, R. H. (1984). The new institutional economics. *Journal of Institutional and Theoretical Economics, 140,* 229–231.

Colander, D., Goldberg, M., Haas, A., Juselius, K., Kirman, A., Lux, T., et al. (2009). The financial crisis and the systemic failure of the economics profession. *Critical Review, 21*(2–3), 249–267. https://doi.org/10.1080/08913810902934109

Cooper, R. (1993). *Winning at new products: Accelerating the process from idea to launch* (2nd ed.). Reading: Addison-Wesley Publishing Company.

Cooper, R., & Edgett, S. (2005). *Lean, rapid and profitable New product development.* Ancaster: Product Development Institute.

Cooper, R., & Kaplan, R. S. (1988a). How cost accounting distorts product cost. *Management Accounting, 69*(10), 20–27.

Cooper, R., & Kaplan, R. S. (1988b). Measure cost right: Making the right decisions. *Harvard Business Review, 65*(5), 96–103.

Dahl, C. F. (2011). Stoltenberg selger 'nordisk modell' i Davos. *Aftenposten.* Retrieved from http://www.aftenposten.no/okonomi/innland/article4010273.ece#.UdriV234V8E

Dahlgaard, J. J., Kristensen, K., Kanji, G. K., Juhl, H. J., & Sohal, A. S. (1998). Quality management practices: A comparative study between east and west. *International Journal of Quality & Reliability Management, 15*(8/9), 812–826.

Denzin, N. K. (1970). *The research act in sociology: A theoretical introduction to sociological methods.* London: Butterworths.

Denzin, N. K. (2009). *The research act: A theoretical introduction to sociological methods.* New Brunswick: Aldine Transaction.

Denzin, N. K., & Lincoln, Y. S. (1994). *Handbook of qualitative research.* Thousand Oaks, CA: Sage.

Descartes: God and Human Nature. (2013). Retrieved from http://www.philosophypages.com/hy/4d.htm

Dosi, G., Nelson, R. R., & Winter, S. G. (2009). *The nature and dynamics of organizational capabilities.* Oxford: Oxford University Press.

ECE. (2010). *EU energy in figures 2010, CO₂ emissions from transport by mode.* Directorate-General for Energy and Transport (DG TREN).

EFFRA. (2013a). *EFFRA: Introduction to our association.* Retrieved from http://www.effra.eu/index.php?option=com_content&view=article&id=122&Itemid=121

EFFRA. (2013b). *Factories of the future: Multi-annual roadmap for the contractual PPP under Horizon 2020.* Retrieved from http://www.effra.eu/index.php?option=com_content&view=category&id=85&Itemid=133

Elster, J. (2007). *Explaining social behavior: More nuts and bolts for the social sciences.* Cambridge: Cambridge University Press.

Ennals, J. R. (2006). Theatre and workplace actors. In B. Göranzon, M. Hammarén, & J. R. Ennals (Eds.), *Dialogue, skill & tacit knowledge* (pp. 307–319). West Sussex: John Wiley & Sons.

Evans-Pritchard, E. E., & Gillies, E. (1976). *Witchcraft, oracles, and magic among the Azande.* Oxford: Oxford University Press.

Flick, U. (1998). *An introduction to qualitative research: Theory, method and applications.* London: Sage.

Flynn, D. K. (2009). "My customers are different!" Identity, difference, and the political economy of design. In M. Cefkin (Ed.), *Ethnography and the corporate encounter: Reflections on research in and of corporations.* New York: Berghahn Books.

Ford-Motor-Company. (2004). *FMEA handbook version 4.1.* Ford Design Institute.

Foss, N., Pedersen, T., Pyndt, J., & Schultz, M. (2012). *Innovating organization and management.* New York: Cambridge University Press.

Freyssenet, M. (2009). *The second automobile revolution – Trajectories of the world carmakers in the 21st century.* New York: Palgrave Macmillan.

Freyssenet, M., Mair, A., Shimizu, K., & Volpato, G. (1998). *One best way? Trajectories and industrial models of the world's automobile producers.* Oxford: Oxford University Press.

Fujimoto, T. (1997). The dynamic aspect of product development capabilities: An international comparison in the automobile industry. In A. Goto & H. Odagiri (Eds.), *Innovation in Japan* (pp. 57–59). Oxford: Oxford University Press.

Fujimoto, T. (1999a). Capability building and over-adaptation: A case of 'fat design' in the Japanese auto industry. In Y. Lung, J.-J. Chanaron, & D. Raff (Eds.), *Coping with variety: Flexible productive systems for product variety in the auto industry* (pp. 261–286). Hampshire: Ashgate Publishing Limited.

Fujimoto, T. (1999b). *The evolution of a manufacturing system at Toyota.* New York: Oxford University Press.

Fuller, S. (2002). *Knowledge management foundations.* Boston, MA: Butterworth-Heinemann.

Garicano, L., & Wu, Y. (2012). Knowledge, communication, and organizational capabilities. *Organization Science, 23*(5), 1382–1397.

Geertz, C. (1973). *The interpretation of cultures.* New York: Basic Books.

Ghoshal, S., & Bartlett, C. A. (1997). *The individualized corporation: A fundamentally new approach to management: Great companies are defined by purpose, process, and people.* New York: Harper Business.

Giuliani, E., & Bell, M. (2005). The micro-determinants of meso-level learning and innovation: Evidence from a Chilean wine cluster. *Research Policy, 34,* 47–68.

Gluckman, M. (1963). *Order and rebellion in tribal Africa: Collected essays with an autobiographical introduction.* London: Cohen & West.

Gluckman, M., Mitchell, J. C., & Barnes, J. A. (1963). The village headman in British Central Africa. In M. Gluckman (Ed.), *Order and rebellion in tribal Africa.* London: Cohen & West.

Göranzon, B., Hammarén, M., & Ennals, J. R. (Eds.). (2004). *Dialogue, skill & tacit knowledge.* West Sussex: John Wiley & Sons.

Gotzamani, K. D., & Tsiotras, G. D. (2001). An empirical study of the ISO 9000 standard's contribution towards total quality management. *International Journal of Operations and Production Management, 21*(10), 1326–1342.

Greenwood, D. J. (1991). Collective reflective practice through participatory action research: A case study from the Fagor cooperatives of Mondragón. In D. Schön (Ed.), *The reflective turn – Case studies in and on educational practice* (pp. 84–108). New York: Teachers College Press.

Greenwood, D. J., & González Santos, J. L. (1992). *Industrial democracy as process: Participatory action research in the Fagor cooperative group of Mondragón.* Assen: Van Gorcum.

Guba, E. G., & Lincoln, Y. S. (1989). *Fourth generation evaluation.* Newbury Park, CA: Sage.

Gulati, R. (2007). *Managing network resources: Alliances, affiliations, and other relational assets.* New York: Oxford University Press.

Gustavsen, B., Finne, H., & Oscarsson, B. (2001). *Creating connectedness: The role of social research in innovation policy.* Amsterdam: John Benjamins Publishing Company.

Harry, M. J., & Schroeder, R. (2000). *Six Sigma: The breakthrough management strategy revolutionizing the world's top corporations.* New York: Currency.

Hirokazu, S., & Hiroshi, N. (2005). Reliability problem prevention method for automotive components-development of GD'3' activity and DRBFM method for stimulating creativity and visualizing problems. *Transaction of Society of Automotive Engineers of Japan, 36*(4), 163–168.

Hirschhorn, L. (1997). *Reworking authority: Leading and following in the post-modern organization.* Cambridge, MA: MIT Press.

Ho, S. K. M. (1995). Is the ISO 9000 series for total quality management. *International Journal of Physical Distribution & Logistics Management, 25*(1), 51–66.

Ho, M. H. C., & Verspagen, B. (2006). The role of national borders and regions in knowledge flows. In E. Lorenz & B. Å. Lundvall (Eds.), *How Europe's economies learn: Coordinating competing models* (pp. 50–79). Oxford: Oxford University Press.

Holtskog, H. (2013a). Continuous improvement beyond the Lean understanding. *Procedia CIRP, 7*(0), 575–579. https://doi.org/10.1016/j.procir.2013.06.035

Holtskog, H. (2013b). Lean and innovative: Two discourses. In H. C. G. Johnsen & E. Pålshaugen (Eds.), *Hva er innovasjon? Perspektiver i norsk innovasjonsforskning. Bind 2: Organisasjon og medvirkning – en norsk modell?* (pp. 45–64). Oslo: Cappelen Damm Akademisk.

Holtskog, H., Martinsen, K., Skogsrød, T., & Ringen, G. (2016). The pivoting problem of Lean. *Procedia CIRP, 41*, 591–595.

Holtskog, H., Ringen, G., & Endrerud, J. O. (2010). *Financial crisis affects absorptive capacity: Case Raufoss cluster.* Paper presented at the 5th International Seminar on Regional Innovation Policies, Grimstad, Norway.

Hutchins, D. C. (2008). *Hoshin Kanri: The strategic approach to continuous improvement.* Aldershot: Gower.

Ichijo, K., & Nonaka, I. (2007). *Knowledge creation and management.* Oxford: Oxford University Press.

IFO-Institute. (2010). *Annual report 2009.* Munich: Verband der Automobilindustrie.

Ingvaldsen, J. A., Holtskog, H., & Ringen, G. (2013). Unlocking work standards through systematic work observation: Implications for team supervision. *Team Performance Management, 19*(5/6), 279–291.

Isaksen, A., & Kalsaas, B. T. (2009). Suppliers and strategies for upgrading in global production networks. The case of a supplier to the global automotive industry in a high-cost location. European Planning Studies, Special Edition.

Jermier, J. M. (1991). Critical epistemology and the study of organizational culture: Reflections on street corner society. In P. J. Frost et al. (Eds.), *Reframing organizational culture* (pp. 223–233). Newbury Park, CA: Sage.

Johnsen, H. (2001). *Involvement at work.* PhD, Copenhagen Business School, Copenhagen.

Johnsen, H. (Ed.). (2012). *A collaborative economic model – The case of Norway.* Farnham: Gower.

Johnsen, H. C. G., & Pålshaugen, E. (2011). *Hva er innovasjon? Perspektiver i Norsk innovasjonsforskning bind 1.* Kristiansand: Høyskoleforlaget.

Johnson, H. T., & Kaplan, R. S. (1987). *Relevance lost: The rise and fall of management accounting.* Boston, MA: Harvard Business School Press.

Kennedy, M. N. (2003). *Product development for the Lean enterprise, why Toyota's system is four times more productive and how you can implement it.* Richmond: The Oaklea Press.

Kesting, P., & Ulhøi, J. P. (2010). Employee-driven innovation: Extending the license to foster innovation. *Management Decisions, 48*(1), 65–84.

Kiella, M. L., & Golhar, D. Y. (1997). Total quality management in an R&D environment. *International Journal of Operations and Production Management, 17*(2), 184–198.

Klein, J. A. (1989, March–April). The human cost of manufacturing reform. *Harvard Business Review*, 60–66.

Klein, J. A. (1991). A reexamination of autonomy in light of new manufacturing practices. *Human Relations, 44*(1), 21–38. https://doi.org/10.1177/001872679104400102

Klemsdal, L. (2008). *Making sense of "the new way of organizing": Managing the micro processes of (planned) change in a municipality* (Vol. 2008:300). Trondheim: Norges teknisk-naturvitenskapelige universitet.

Klev, R., & Levin, M. (2009). *Forandring som praksis: endringsledelse gjennom læring og utvikling*. Bergen: Fagbokforl.

Kunda, G. (2006). *Engineering culture: Control and commitment in a high-tech corporation*. Philadelphia, PA: Temple University Press.

Kushner, H. S. (1981). *When bad things happen to good people*. New York: Schocken Books.

Lee, J., Bagheri, B., & Kao, H. (2015). A cyber-physical systems architecture for industry 4-0-based manufacturing systems. *Manufacturing Letters, 3*, 18–23.

Lee, J., Kao, H., & Yang, S. (2014). Service innovation and smart analytics for industry 4.0 and big data environment. *Procedia CIRP, 16*, 3–8.

Lehrer, J. (2012). *Imagine: How creativity works*. Boston, MA: Houghton Mifflin Harcourt.

Levinthal, D. A. (2009). Organizational capabilities in complex worlds. In G. Dosi, P. R. Nelson, & S. G. Winter (Eds.), *The nature and dynamics of organizational capabilities* (pp. 363–379). Oxford: Oxford University Press.

Liker, J. (2004). *The Toyota way: 14 management principles from the world's greatest manufacturer*. New York: McGraw-Hill.

Liker, J. (2007). *Tools & technology*. Presentation. Gardermoen, Oslo.

Liker, J., & Hoseus, M. (2008). *Toyota culture: The heart and soul of the Toyota way*. New York: McGraw-Hill.

Lodgaard, E., Larsson, C. E., & Ringen, G. (2013). *Viewing the engineering change process from a Lean product development and a business perspective*. Not yet published.

Lukes, S. (2005). *Power: A radical view*. Basingstoke: Palgrave Macmillan.

Mair, A. (1998). The globalization of Honda's product-led flexible mass production system. In M. Freyssenet, A. Mair, K. Shimizu, & G. Volpato (Eds.), *One best way?* (pp. 110–138). Oxford: Oxford University Press.

ManuFuture A Vision for 2020. (2004). Retrieved from http://www.manufuture.org/wp-content/uploads/manufuture_vision_en1.pdf

Martin, J. (1992). *Cultures in organizations: Three perspectives*. New York: Oxford University Press.

Miles, H., & Huberman, M. (1994). *Qualitative data analysis: A sourcebook*. Beverly Hills, CA: Sage.

Moaveni, S. (2003). *Finite element analysis: Theory and application with ANSYS*. Upper Saddle River, NJ: Pearson Education.

Morgan, J., & Liker, J. K. (2006). *The Toyota product development system, integrating people, process and technology*. New York: Productivity Press.

Morse, J. (2010). Procedures and practice of mix method design: Maintaining control, rigor, and complexity. In A. Tashakkori & C. Teddlie (Eds.), *SAGE handbook of mixed methods in social & behavioral research* (pp. 339–352). Thousand Oaks, CA: Sage.

Nelson, R. R., & Winter, S. G. (1982). *An evolutionary theory of economic change.* Cambridge, MA: Harvard University Press.

Niosi, J. (2012). *Building national and regional innovation systems: Institutions for economic development.* New York: Edward Elgar Publishing.

Nishiguchi, T. E. (1996). *Managing product development.* New York: Oxford University Press.

Nonaka, I. (1994). A dynamic theory of organizational knowledge creation. *Organization Science, 5*(1), 14–37.

Nonaka, I., & Nishiguchi, T. (2001). *Knowledge emergence – Social, technical, and evolutionary dimensions of knowledge creation.* New York: Oxford University Press.

Oakland, J. S. (2003). *Total quality management: Text with cases.* Amsterdam: Butterworth-Heinemann.

OECD. (2007). *OECD territorial reviews Norway.* Paris: Organisation for Economic Cooperation and Development.

Ohno, T. (1978). *The Toyota production system.* Tokyo: Diamond.

Ohno, T. (1988). *Toyota production system: Beyond large-scale production.* New York: Productivity Press.

Ottosson, S. (2010). *Frontline innovation management – Dynamic product & business development.* Stockholm: Ottosson & Partners.

Patton, M. Q. (2002). *Qualitative research & evaluation methods.* Beverly Hills, CA: Sage.

Pedersen, S. H. (2012). *Employee-driven innovation: A new approach.* Basingstoke: Palgrave Macmillan.

Polanyi, M. (1958). *Personal knowledge.* Chicago, IL: The University of Chicago Press.

Polanyi, M. (1966). *The Tacit dimension.* London: Routledge & Kegan Paul.

Powell, T. C. (1995). Total quality management as competitive advantage: A review and empirical study. *Strategic Management Journal, 16*, 15–37.

Pyzdek, T., & Keller, P. A. (2010). *The Six Sigma handbook: A complete guide for green belts, black belts, and managers at all levels.* New York: McGraw-Hill.

Ringen, G. (2010). *Organizational learning and knowledge in the Norwegian automotive supplier industry.* Doctor philosophiae, NTNU, Trondheim.

Ringen, G., & Holtskog, H. (2009). *Product development in the financial crisis.* Paper presented at the ICED, Stanford University, USA.

Ringen, G., Holtskog, H., & Endrerud, J. O. (2009). *How the automotive and financial crisis affect innovations in an industrial cluster?* Paper presented at the 3rd ISPIM Innovation Symposium, Quebec City, Canada.

Røvik, K. A. (1998). *Moderne organisasjoner: trender i organisasjonstenkningen ved tusenårsskiftet.* Bergen-Sandviken: Fagbokforl.

Roy, D. F. (1959). Banana Time: Job satisfaction and informal interaction. *Human Organization, 18,* 158–168.

Scharff, J. S., & Scharff, D. E. (2005). *The legacy of Fairbairn and Sutherland: Psychotherapeutic applications.* London: Routledge.

Schuh, G., Potente, T., Wesch-Potente, C., Weber, A., & Prote, J. (2014). Collaboration mechanisms to increase productivity in the context of industrie 4.0. *Procedia CIRP, 19,* 51–56.

Scott, J. (1997). *Corporate business and capitalist classes.* Oxford: Oxford University Press.

Segal, J. (1992). *Melanie Klein.* London: Sage.

Sennett, R. (2008). *The craftsman.* New Haven, CT: Yale University Press.

Shankar, P., Morkos, B., & Summers, J. D. (2012). Reasons for change propagation: A case study in an automotive OEM. *Research in Engineering, 23,* 291–303.

Shimizu, K. (1995). Humanization of the production system and work at Toyota Motor Co and Toyota Motor Kyushu. In Å. Sandberg (Ed.), *Enriching production – Perspectives on Volvo's Uddevalla plant as an alternative to Lean production* (pp. 383–404). Aldershot: Ashgate Publishing.

Shimizu, K. (1998). A new Toyotaism. In M. Freyssenet, A. Mair, K. Shimizu, & G. Volpato (Eds.), *One best way?* (pp. 63–90). Oxford: Oxford University Press.

Shimokawa, K., & Fujimoto, T. (2010). *The birth of Lean.* Cambridge, MA: Lean Enterprise Institute.

Shook, J. (2008). *Managing to learn: Using A3 management process to solve problems.* Cambridge: Lean Enterprise Institute.

Simon, H. (1972). Theories of bounded rationality. In C. B. McGuire & R. Radner (Eds.), *Decision and organization.* Amsterdam: North-Holland Publishing Company.

Simon, H. (1982). *Models of bounded rationality* (Vols. 1–2). Cambridge, MA: MIT Press.

Smith, M., & Kleine, P. (1986). Qualitative research and evaluation: Triangulation and multimethods reconsidered. In D. Williams (Ed.), *Naturalistic evaluation (New directions for program evaluation).* San Francisco: Jossey-Bass.

Sobek, D. K., & Smalley, A. (2008). *Understanding A3 thinking: A critical component of Toyota's PDCA management system.* New York: Productivity Press.

Steward, M. (2009). RIP, MBA. *CNBC.com.* Retrieved from http://www.cnbc.com/id/29895258

Stiglitz, J. E. (2009). The anatomy of a murder: Who killed America's economy? *Critical Review, 21*(2–3), 329–339. https://doi.org/10.1080/08913810902934133

Taguchi, G., & Clausing, D. (1990). Robust quality. *Harvard Business Review, 68*(1), 65–75.

Taguchi, G., Elsayed, E. A., & Hsiang, T. C. (1989). *Quality engineering in production systems*. New York: McGraw-Hill.

Tashakkori, A., & Teddlie, C. (2010). *SAGE handbook of mixed methods in social & behavioral research*. Thousand Oaks, CA: Sage.

Taylor, F. W. (1911). *The principles of scientific management*. New York: Harper & Brothers.

Teknikföretagen. (2015). *Made i Sweden 2030*. Retrieved from https://www.teknikforetagen.se/globalassets/i-debatten/publikationer/produktion/made-in-sweden-2030-engelsk.pdf

Turing, A. (1950). Computing machinery and intelligence. *Mind, 59*(236), 433–460.

Von Krogh, G., Ichijo, K., & Nonaka, I. (2000). *Enabling knowledge creation. How to unlock the mystery of tacit knowledge and release the power of innovation*. Oxford: Oxford University Press.

Weick, K. E. (1995). *Sensemaking in organizations*. London: Sage.

Why Economists Failed to Predict the Financial Crisis. Knowledge@Wharton (2009, May 13). Retrieved from http://knowledge.wharton.upenn.edu/article/why-economists-failed-to-predict-the-financial-crisis/

Whyte, W. F. (1949). The social structure of the restaurant. *American Journal of Sociology, 54*, 302–310.

Williamson, O. (1979). Transaction-cost economics: The governance of contractual relations. *Journal of Law & Economics, 22*(2), 233–261.

Williamson, O. (1985). *The economic institutions of capitalism*. New York: The Free Press.

Williamson, O. (1991). Comparative economic organization: The analysis of discrete structural alternatives. *Administrative Science Quarterly, 36*(2), 269–296.

Williamson, O. (1996). *The mechanisms of governance*. New York: Oxford University Press.

Womack, J. P., & Jones, D. T. (1996). *Lean thinking: Banish waste and create wealth in your corporation*. New York: Free Press.

Womack, J. P., Jones, D. T., & Roos, D. (1990). *The machine that changed the world: Based on the Massachusetts Institute of Technology 5-million dollar 5-year study on the future of the automobile*. New York: Rawson Associates.

Yeasmin, S., & Rahman, K. F. (2012). 'Triangulation' research method as the tool of social science research. *BUP Journal, 1*(1), 154–163.

Zanarini, M. C., Weingeroff, J. L., & Frankenburg, F. R. (2009). Defense mechanisms associated with borderline personality disorder. *Journal of Personality Disorder, 23*(2), 113–121.

INDEX[1]

---

[1] Note: Page number followed by "n" refers to notes.

© The Author(s) 2018   167

H. Holtskog et al., *Learning Factories*, Palgrave Studies in Democracy, Innovation, and Entrepreneurship for Growth, https://doi.org/10.1007/978-3-319-41887-2

CPSIA information can be obtained
at www.ICGtesting.com
Printed in the USA
LVOW13*1745301017

554317LV00013B/364/P